Praise for *Le*

"Frank Biondi is the type of leader you want on your team. I speak from experience; we played baseball together at Princeton. *Let's Be Frank* offers timeless lessons about how to make your own contributions to the world, just as Frank did for the media industry and the friends, colleagues, and communities he lifted up during his life."

—Former U.S. Senator **BILL BRADLEY**, author of *We Can All Do Better*

"A lovely and deserved portrait of Frank Biondi. . . . He became one of my go-to executives as I strove to understand the fast-changing media business. I greatly valued our relationship and his knowledge. Like many in business, he had talent. But he also had something all too rare: decency."

—**KEN AULETTA**, *New York Times* best-selling author of *Googled*

"The life of Frank Biondi shows what true principle and integrity can mean in a field where it's not always present."

—**NORMAN LEAR**, legendary television and movie producer
and author of *Even This I Get to Experience*

"Attention to detail, moral compass, humility; these are characteristics that describe Frank Biondi and his long tenure as an outstanding entertainment executive. And, by the way, Sumner Redstone said to me that 'hiring Frank was a fantastic move and firing him was my biggest mistake.'"

—**MICHAEL EISNER**, former chairman and CEO of the
Walt Disney Company and author of *Working Together:
Why Great Partnerships Succeed*

"I had the privilege to know Frank both as a top business executive and as a friend. In both roles, he comported himself with the same combination of intelligence, humility, and total integrity. I'm so glad that through this book, he will be remembered as he is deserved to be."

—STEVE RATTNER, chairman and CEO of Willett Advisors, economic analyst on MSNBC's *Morning Joe*, former counselor to the Secretary of the Treasury and author of *Overhaul*

"Frank Biondi had an extraordinary impact on my life and my career. The lessons imparted in *Let's Be Frank* are timeless and remind me of what a remarkable leader and person he was. Frank outlines to the reader how to carve out your own path, learning from the leaders of the past, just as he did."

—JIM STEYER, Founder of Common Sense Media, professor at Stanford University, and author of *Which Side of History*

"Get ready to learn from one of the most influential people you've never heard of. Although Frank Biondi had a monumental impact on the world of entertainment, he preferred to stay out of the spotlight. At long last, this book takes you backstage to see how he led many of Hollywood's most iconic brands, made decisions, and built relationships."

—ADAM GRANT, #1 *New York Times* bestselling author of *Think Again* and host of the TED podcast *WorkLife*

FRANK BIONDI WITH JANE BIONDI MUNNA

Let's Be
Frank

A DAUGHTER'S TRIBUTE TO HER FATHER,

THE MEDIA MOGUL YOU'VE NEVER HEARD OF

RIVER GROVE
BOOKS

This book is a memoir reflecting the authors' truthful recollections of experiences over time. Except where noted, the story and words are the authors' alone. Some details and characteristics may have been changed, the chronology of some events may have been compressed, and some dialogue may have been recreated and/or supplemented.

Published by River Grove Books
Austin, TX
www.rivergrovebooks.com

Grateful acknowledgment is made to the following source(s) for permission to reproduce copyrighted material:
Photo of Frank Biondi and peers for *Vanity Fair*: Annie Leibovitz / Trunk Archive: Photography copyright ©Annie Leibovitz.
Wired cover copyright ©John Plunkett; concept and design: John Plunkett; Photoshop imagery: Eugene Mosier.

Distributed by River Grove Books

Design and composition by Greenleaf Book Group and Brian Phillips
Cover design by Greenleaf Book Group and Brian Phillips
Cover images copyright Igor Shikov and Phongphan. Used under license from Shutterstock.com; ©iStockphoto.com/Extreme Media, 2019; ©Willem Arriens/Alamy Stock Photo; ©Mark Waugh/Alamy Stock Photo; ©Kristoffer Tripplaar/Alamy Stock Photo.

Publisher's Cataloging-in-Publication data is available.

Print ISBN: 978-1-63299-579-7

eBook ISBN: 978-1-63299-580-3

First Edition

Nothing made Frank happier than being
"Poppi" to his incredible grandchildren.
This book is dedicated to them: Diana, Charlotte,
Katherine, Victoria, Bobby, and Maisie.
He loved you so much!

Special Thanks

Given Frank passed away before the book was finished, the time and perspective of his devoted former colleagues and friends made it possible to finish what he started. Special thanks to Jim Stein, without whom you would not be reading this. Jim's guidance, expertise, friendship, and encouragement over many years made this entire endeavor possible.

Thank you does not quite capture the full gratitude owed to Alan Horn, Alan Schwartz, Greg Meidel, Henry Schleiff, Jon Dolgen, Ken Solomon, Martin Shafer, Dr. Phil McGraw, Rick Reiss, Scott Budnick, Sherry Lansing, and Tom Freston for their time, input, and commitment to this book. Thanks also to Peter Chernin, Rob Reiner, Neil Braun, and Bill Robinson for letting me share their remembrances within the book.

Thanks to Jeff Wilser for his work with my father and me to turn his life experiences and recordings into engaging written stories.

Personal thanks to my husband for his support and encouragement across the years from idea to completion with so much in between.

The final and most special thanks goes to my mom, Carol, for her encouragement and assistance with this multiyear project, but even more for her belief and support of my father throughout their forty-five years of marriage. She encouraged (and pushed!) him to be his best and reach the highest heights in life and in business.

Contents

An Unsung Mogul

FRANK

My wife, Carol, is very active in dealing with children who are in the child welfare system and the juvenile justice system. In the course of that work, she bumped into a young man who was also helping kids who were incarcerated. The young man's name was Scott Budnick, who happened to work at Warner Bros. as a producer.

So we would all socialize from time to time. One day I said to Scott, just to make conversation, "What's your next movie?"

"Well, we're doing a comedy in Las Vegas."

"What's it about?" I asked.

"It's kind of complicated," he said.

"Where are you in the process?"

"We're just setting up. We won't start for several months."

Now at the time—the mid-2000s—I sat on the board of Harrah's, which ultimately was renamed to Caesars Entertainment.

"Where are you guys going to stay?" I asked Scott.

"I don't know."

"Would you be interested in staying at Caesars, or one of the other Harrah's hotels?"

"Sure, if we can work it out!"

I said, "Let me give the president of Caesars a call."

So I called up the president of Caesars and put the two of them in touch. They were able to make the arrangements and logistics work, and Scott's team stayed in the hotel for three or four months while shooting the film in Vegas.

What I didn't know at the time was that the movie Scott was working on was *The Hangover*.

JANE

That's how my father, Frank Biondi, tells the story of how *The Hangover* came to be made at Caesars Palace in Las Vegas. It's a very Frank story: Dad understates his importance to this story and downplays the significance of his role.

Scott Budnick himself sets the record straight. "I told Frank that we were going to shoot *The Hangover* in Vegas, but we had been denied by The Wynn. We had been denied by Sheldon Adelson [former CEO of The Sands, which also owned The Venetian]. And I think we had just been denied by the MGM group," says Scott. "Literally, it was all hopes for Caesars Palace. And I didn't go in there with an agenda. I didn't know Frank was on the Caesars Board."

It's possible that *The Hangover* doesn't end up as the movie it became without the green light from Caesars, and clearly the hotel was crucial to its success. "I mean, it was a character in the film," says Scott. "It was as important as our actors. It *was* the film. And that's why you see it now as one of the hottest hotels in all of Vegas."

Thanks to the hook-up from my father, says Scott, Caesars gave them unfettered access, which allowed them to pursue their zaniest of comedic stunts. "No matter what we wanted to do, they would always find a way to get to a yes," Scott says, even if it's "crazier shit after crazier shit" like "Mike Tyson knocking them out in a suite."

The MGMs of the world said no. Thanks to my father paying it forward, Caesars said yes. And as you'll see throughout this book, his minor but crucial involvement had an outsized impact on millions of people who would never know his name.

The Investment Banker Who Became a Hollywood Mogul

JANE

I suppose that every little girl grows up admiring her father and learning from his lessons. I know I did. I was his youngest daughter and he called me Janie, or Jane-O. He taught me things that all dads teach their daughters—basic fairness, right and wrong, how to catch a fly ball. (Dad played baseball in college, and still holds a spot in Princeton's record books for stolen bases in a season and a game.)

As a child, I didn't know what, exactly, he did when he went to work, but I could understand that he worked with Big Bird and Snufflcupagus at the Children's Television Workshop, he brought home green slime from Nickelodeon, and we went to the MTV Video Music Awards twenty-five years ago, before it was a phenomenon. I knew he did something with numbers (later learning he started out as an investment banker). For most of my upbringing, I thought the things my father did at work—and the lessons he taught me—were commonplace. *Every kid learns this stuff. Every dad's job is special in some way.*

I would eventually realize that my father's job was highly unusual, and the lessons he taught me were not commonplace in corporate America. Not everyone's dad had been the CEO of HBO, Universal Studios, and Viacom—which also put him in charge of Paramount, MTV, Nickelodeon, Blockbuster, and Simon & Schuster. Not everyone's dad served on twenty corporate boards, from The Bank of New York and Vail Resorts to Hasbro, StubHub, Cablevision, and Madison Square Garden.

And as I grew older, I began to sense the enormous impact my father had on the media industry. In the '80s, at HBO, he had a belief that certain customers would be willing to pay for quality entertainment content. At the time that was hard to believe, almost heretical, but now it's a foundation of the economic model for television, movies, and even social media and digital platforms. I like to joke that my dad was like the Forrest Gump of media—but with smarts and agency—in that he seemed to be a part of every major media development in the early '80s into the '90s—from the consolidation of media conglomerates, to the supremacy of content and the rise and fall of Blockbuster, even serving at the helm of the company that released, well, *Forrest Gump* and many other memorable and important movies.

I had a unique vantage point to witness how my father helped shape the modern entertainment industry. He was modest and never went out of his way to drop names, but he rubbed shoulders with many famous people during his career both inside and outside the entertainment industry. Over the years, he would tell us stories such as how he played tennis against Donald Trump . . . and how his shot literally knocked Trump down to win the match (more on this in chapter 9). He worked directly with people like billionaire media mogul Sumner Redstone, Carl Icahn, Barry Diller, Don King, Alan Horn, Rob Reiner, daytime television icon Merv Griffin, and *Lord of the Rings* director Peter Jackson.

Telling the Untold Stories

JANE

Dad had many stories about his experiences from his career, and I was surprised throughout my life that very few of them were in the press. The reason was simple—my father was all substance, no flair, and he stayed out of the spotlight. Yet the insiders knew that he launched careers, brokered deals behind the scenes, and quietly made things happen.

When Dad told these stories, people always told him, "You should write a book!" His response was always the same. "When Sumner [Redstone] dies." As you'll see in later chapters, Dad had conflicting feelings about Redstone, who both hired and fired him. Dad was grateful for the life-changing opportunity Redstone gave him, but angry and resentful (though secretly relieved!) about how he was let go. The stories about Redstone in this book are some of the few that reflect poorly on the people mentioned, because of my father's low opinion of Redstone's character.

Dad's vow to wait changed in 2018. He had fought many battles in his life, and won most of them, but then he faced an adversary stronger than he had ever faced before: cancer.

And as he faced his mortality, he opened up in a way he hadn't before. And he began writing a book to share his stories and the principles that led to his success. He was committed to making this book happen, so throughout his treatments he would sit down and let me record him telling the stories he wanted to include.

"My first encounter with serendipity was my senior year in high school," he began one day, sharing a story about how he ended up attending Princeton. We first started recording ten days after a major surgery he underwent. He wore a bathrobe, with tubes coming out of multiple places in his body. His kidneys weren't working. I knew he was physically uncomfortable and at times in pain, but there were moments when he lit up, a gleam in his eye, telling me about the time he met Merv Griffin, or how in the middle of intense and high-stakes negotiations, Alan Schwartz mistook the photo of my sister as his own daughter. (You'll read more about all these stories later in the book.)

Listening to him tell these stories gave me a peek inside his life before I was born, or when I was too young to have understood his life outside of our home. He would only record the stories if I was there with him, pressing record on the iPad app. I kept trying to show him how to do it, that it was easy. He wasn't interested. This was something we were doing together and he wanted me there. There were times I traveled to be with him to spend time and record more stories, but he didn't have the energy or the interest. Most of the time he pushed himself to do it anyway. We had stories to get through, and nobody knew how much time we had left.

The stories shed light on his life before our family, the way he thought through opportunities and challenges in both his business and personal lives. And they showed me the origins and connections he had with other important people in his life. As he was dying I was able to share his own stories with the people they featured, a final tribute to long friendships and a life well-lived. His good friend Jon Dolgen, for example, visited my father at home just before he passed. Dad could no longer speak, so I played Jon and his wife the recording of "Expect the Unexpected" (featuring Jon, see chapter 5), and it moved him to tears.

Hearing his stories brought to life the principles that I knew he embodied and the lessons he taught me during my life: doing the work, living with integrity, finding value. Dad found and generated value in so many ways—the value of original content, the value of companies and their discounted cash flows, but also the value of a good joke, the value of a smile, the value of a clean forehand winner, the value of lifelong friends and the family he loved.

The lessons from these stories showed me how Dad maintained his soul while becoming an über-successful businessman in an often soulless industry. And that's why this book is organized around the principles that guided his every action throughout his life.

His simple principles have also helped me process and grieve his loss. I find that I can now imagine his reaction to any given situation or hear his patient advice for helping me navigate a new circumstance.

He taught me to control what you can control, and then embrace and accept the things you can't. Then go one level deeper. If you *can* control something—like outreading everyone else on your team before a big meeting, or understanding the minutiae of discount rates, or even just showing up when you say you're going to show up—that will set you apart from the bulk of the world. Mastering the basics can give you an edge.

Carrying the Torch

JANE

Dad passed away before he could finish this book. (And, ironically, Sumner Redstone passed away just nine months later.)

Soon after, I picked up the baton to help him finish what he started. And I asked some of his friends and former colleagues to share their perspectives so we could fill in a few gaps. That's why this book is a compilation of his stories in his own words, my own perspective, and tributes from friends who shared portions of his life.

At heart, this book is not only about how to be a successful leader—although Dad covers that extensively—but how to be a good person. It's about how to lead a good, fulfilling life. My father is proof that nice guys can finish first, and I view this book as a marriage of his strategies and values, offering some light during dark times.

Deep down, I knew that success at the highest levels of Hollywood is not, at its core, what made my father special. There are other CEOs. There are many moguls. What set my father apart was the way he conducted himself and his approach to business—he did what he did without sacrificing his values or his priorities. He lived his life on his own terms, always. That, to him, was the ultimate definition of success.

I have dedicated the past few years to completing the book as a way to share his stories, honor his legacy, and inspire readers of all stripes—entrepreneurs, business leaders, young professionals, *future* business leaders—to work well, to thrive, to live and laugh and love, and, well, to be like Frank.

CHAPTER 1

Seize Your Destiny

JANE

Dad's forty-year career in media (1960s to early 2000s) spanned the birth of pay television to the advent of streaming content, from the mainstreaming of cable to the seeds of vertical integration of media content and distribution. In a far shorter time frame, Netflix launched in 1997, then evolved from mailing DVDs in red envelopes (competing with Blockbuster) to developing its own content—and streaming their massive content library—to a larger subscriber audience than all the other streaming services.

Most of my father's stories are set in the media world of the '70s, '80s, and '90s, which, at first glance, can feel like a different universe compared to today, filled with TV antennas, fax machines, and cell phones the size of an iron. But if you read closely, you'll see that the challenges he describes are just as relevant in the 2020s as they were in the 1960s–1990s. The "streaming wars" are simply the latest chapter in a story that my father helped begin, nearly half a century ago. He was the right man at the right time for many of the innovations that came along and seized every opportunity to push the boundaries of TV and movies into the future.

To give you a preview of the events, people, and decisions that you'll see in this book, this chapter provides a quick history of TV and film content distribution and walks through some highlights of Dad's career during those four decades.

A Brief History: From Broadcast to Streaming Content

JANE

In the 1960s, a hot new technology threatened to disrupt the dominance long enjoyed by NBC and the other major television broadcast networks: cable. The early days were fractured. "There were 640 local systems . . . serving some 650,000 subscribers," explains Megan Mullen in *Television in the Multichannel Age*, one of the few books on the subject. These local systems merged. Bigger players gobbled up the smaller ones, hoping to expand their customer base and compete with the broadcast networks.

The largest of these cable companies was called TelePrompTer— think of it as an early Comcast or Spectrum (and clearly the cable company with the oddest use of capital letters). The scramble to scoop up cable companies meant that you would need to figure out how much these companies were worth, which is exactly what my father did as an investment banker. At the time, TelePrompTer was a high-flying growth company, threatening to change the way that millions of Americans watched their TV.

And as far back as the 1950s, cable companies dabbled in direct pay-for-content, foreshadowing the streaming models to come. (One company, called International Telemeter, even experimented with using a coin-box device for customers to buy content). A company that began as the "Green Channel" in 1969 suggested a pay-per-content service focused on movies and sports. The Green Channel would soon change its name to Home Box Office, or just HBO for short.

Adoption continued. In a period of explosive growth known as "Blue Sky," new satellite technology helped expand the reach of cable to more cable systems around the country, without relying on more cable along the ground. Cable systems reached 4.5 million subscribers in 1970. (For context, today there are over seventy-five million US subscribers to Netflix alone.) But this would be a double-edged sword, as cable companies would—eventually—grapple with the threat of new players beaming content directly to consumers' households, such as EchoStar/DISH and DIRECTV.

In the late '70s and '80s, we would see the rise of channels like CSPAN, ESPN, MTV, and of course HBO—all on the hunt for compelling content that could compete with broadcast television. My father had a hand in much of this, as you'll see in the career highlights below and the stories later in this book.

The point of all of this? Today, in what's often referred to as the Streaming Wars, the big players like Netflix, Amazon, Disney, and Hulu are in a race to create their own original content, which frees them from the financial yoke of licensing fees, and it also helps them lure in new subscribers. This is not a new strategy. My father worked on this for decades. "Disney, ViacomCBS, and others all face the same dilemma: While their futures are tied to streaming, their current profits are tied to businesses in terminal decline—theaters and traditional television," noted an Axios media trend report in 2020, on the heels of Warner Bros. announcing they would stream all of their 2021 movies directly to HBO Max.

While the rise of streaming feels like a meteor crashing into the planet of cable TV and movie theaters—something new, something big, something unprecedented—on the other hand, this is the same kind of disruption that cable threw at broadcast TV back in those early days. The technology might change, but the themes are timeless. The media stories of the past can help us brace for the media stories of tomorrow.

As it happens, my father had unique insight into almost every inflection point of this journey, as he helped drive the change and even anticipated the future. He recognized and seized opportunities when they came his way. To paint the backdrop of what was going on during his working years and the role that he played, here are some highlights from Dad's career, beginning when he was a high school student.

A Lucky High School Student goes to Princeton (Early 1960s)

JANE

My father returned to this story often, as he never lost sight of his good fortune, and how it would have a ripple effect throughout his life and career.

FRANK

Throughout my business career, I came to discover that serendipity played a large role in my success.

My first encounter with serendipity was in my senior year in high school, where I had applied to two colleges: Lehigh University, which my father had attended, and Princeton, which I greatly admired.

Now, Lehigh is largely an engineering school, and even back then, I was more interested in business. It turned out that when my father was a student at Lehigh, his advisor had now become the university's president. So when I went to visit Lehigh, of course we went to see the president. And the president sort of announced, casually, that I was admitted.

I told him I was happy to hear that. I also told him that I was interested in playing college baseball, since I was an accomplished player. At the time I thought I could maybe go pro, and this wasn't quite as starry-eyed as it sounds; I was our team captain, made All-State, and was later inducted into the Livingston High School Hall of Fame.

"You'll soon hear from the coach," the president assured me, and we parted ways feeling very good about the proposition, so much so that I withdrew my application to Princeton in the winter of 1962.

Now as fate would have it, my father had several charitable endeavors, and he chaired the ward of a hospital in Orange, New Jersey. This was a tough town, but the hospital had a very patrician, old-line board of directors. And the board had some influential figures. Two of the directors were Whitney Landon, who was a vice president at AT&T, and Brian Leeb, a vice president at Bankers Trust Company.

These two directors, apparently, were interested in my baseball career. They asked my father where I was going to school. He told them that I had pretty much committed to Lehigh, but I still had yet to hear from the baseball coach.

"He's going to study engineering?" they asked my father, knowing Lehigh was renowned for its engineering program.

"No, he's going to study business."

The two men thought for a moment. "Do you think he would be open to coming down and having lunch with us one afternoon?" they asked my father.

"Well, I'll ask him," my father said.

So my father relayed all of this to me. I didn't know exactly what they wanted to talk about, but I agreed to meet them for lunch and hear what they had to say.

Both Whitney and Brian lived in a community known as Llewellyn Park. Even then, Llewellyn Park was very much a throwback. It's a private gated community, and when you step through these gates you travel back in time. Each house was massive. The homes were well-manicured, had lots of staff, and the one thing I remember most was the white-jacketed African American waiters serving our lunch. This was something I had never seen growing up, except maybe in the movies.

Whitney and Brian were very polite, asking me nice questions about why I was interested in business, what I thought I could accomplish, and what I saw in my future.

Finally, at the end of the meal, they looked at me and said, "To be totally candid with you, if you really want to get a great business program, the way to do it is to go to a great undergraduate liberal arts school, and then get a master's in business administration at another fine university."

"Okay," I said. "Let's say I accept what you are telling me. The only problem is that there is a great undergraduate liberal arts school— Princeton—but I withdrew my application."

In yet another coincidence, these two men were also both trustees of Princeton University. And when I expressed my puzzlement, the biggest grins crossed their faces. "Don't misinterpret what we're about to tell you," they said, "but we can, with reasonable certainty, assure you that your application will be reinstated."

For context, this lunch happened in March of 1962. That's well past the normal cut-offs for applications, as colleges issued their acceptances in early April, just weeks away.

"If you can do it," I said, "I would be very appreciative."

"Don't misunderstand," they said again. "This doesn't mean you're going to get in, but it does mean you will get in the mix."

Wind the clock forward twenty days. I was about to play an away game—one of my final games for the Livingston High School baseball team. I was sitting on the team bus, and the bus was about to leave.

A car pulled up. It was my mother's car. She jumped out and handed me an envelope through the window of the bus. The letter was from Princeton University. It essentially said: *We are pleased to announce that you have been accepted to the class of 1966.*

This was probably the most significant decision that I made in my very young career. Much later, in hindsight, it taught me to appreciate the serendipity of who you knew, who cared about you, and the lucky bounces that came your way. And I'll always be grateful, as it probably changed the direction of my life forever and led me to pay it forward for others whenever I had the opportunity.

An Investment Banker & the Broken Toys, Part 1 (1968–1972)

JANE

Dad went on to study at Harvard Business School, graduating in 1968, after which he got the first of his three jobs in investment banking during the 1968–1972 time frame. Dad's experiences in this field were the foundation for many of the lessons and principles you'll read about later in the book.

In legal dramas like *Erin Brockovich* or *A Civil Action*, typically there are big, important moments that make it clear who's in the right and who's in the wrong. But in real life it's usually trickier to spot. In this story from the earliest part of Dad's career, he shows the importance of following through when something doesn't feel right.

FRANK

In one of my first jobs after graduating from Harvard Business School, in 1968, I joined the firm of Cogan, Berlind, Weill & Levitt—the original investment banking firm of Sandy Weill, who later became the CEO of Citigroup. It was a start-up of around two hundred people, and I was only the second investment banker they hired.

Back then, around the office, you'd constantly hear about the private investment that most of the senior partners had made in a toy company in Elizabeth, New Jersey, named Topper Toys.

Topper was a real player in the industry. They had a number of successful toys such as "Johnny Lightning," which gave Mattel's Hot Wheels a run for its money. The company had some heat. And Topper had just emerged from a refinancing of sorts, and our firm had helped them to recapitalize, so we already had a relationship. All the partners at the firm (Cogan, Berlind, Weill, and Levitt) were excited about the day when it would go public.

About a year after I'd been hired, Topper announced that they would file a registration statement, a first step in becoming a public company. By then we expanded the investment banking department by six or seven principals. Conrad Steric (the newest partner in investment banking) was assigned to handle the deal, and I was the junior guy helping out.

None of us knew anything about the toy industry. But after some basic due diligence, it became apparent that: 1) it was a "hits" business; and 2) the retailers had something called "universal rights of return." This meant that the toy retailers, Topper Toys' customers, could return any toys at will.

As we began to dig into the details, we learned that all the other toy companies (Mattel, Hasbro, and so on) acknowledged that the retailers had "universal rights of return," but Topper insisted that they—unlike the rest of the industry—had a no return policy. This seemed strange. Why did Topper get to be different? And this was tough to confirm, as we were not allowed to talk to any of Topper's retail customers—a fiat from Topper's chief executive.

As time went on, the rest of the due diligence was fairly straight-forward. Topper had one plant—or really more of a distribution center—in Elizabeth, New Jersey. It wasn't a giant company. The due diligence wasn't complicated. But we became somewhat obsessed with what seemed like an arcane question: *How could they, realistically, have a no return policy when they were a relatively small player in the Industry and all the other players did it differently?* Something felt fishy.

Now compounding that, we learned that Topper had decided to sponsor the race car driver Al Unser at the upcoming Indianapolis 500. They branded the car as the "Johnny Lightning Special," driven by Al Unser. The car was bright blue with yellow lightning bolts. But the timing complicated things, as it looked like our effective date of Topper Toys' public offering was going to be right around the Indy 500. The problem: The Securities and Exchange Commission (SEC) requires a "quiet period" before an IPO that forbids publicity so as not to influence the value of a stock artificially. Nothing about the Indianapolis 500 is "quiet." So we called the SEC and asked, "What happens if Unser wins?"

A long pause.

They eventually said, "Let's see if he wins, then we'll talk to you."

Well as luck would have it, of course Al Unser won. And the SEC said to us, effectively, "You're going to have to postpone the offering for two weeks, to let the publicity die down." We postponed it, and of course the stock market just happened to nosedive.

Meanwhile, we kept scratching our heads about that return policy. We kicked around the idea that we were able to underwrite, if you will—or prove with their accounting ledgers—that although the company said they didn't take returns, they actually did, and they were able to do it with an accounting treatment that forced the customer to overorder for the next year; they were then netting the returns against the volume for the following year.

Enter the auditor for Topper's listing on the NYSE who insisted that these accounting entries didn't work. We had him over, and in fact, we were right. It *could* work. They conceded the point and said, "Okay, we'll do a special revenue audit. We'll take two or three weeks, and we'll go back and relook at the revenues and prove the deal one way or the other."

A few weeks rolled by. They came back rather smugly and basically said, "Nice try. The arithmetic would've worked, but that's not what's going on." They said the revenues were as they had indicated in the financial statements and signed off on them.

We prepared to go public in May. But something still didn't feel right about this, and Conrad Steric (the partner from Cogan, Berlind, Weill & Levitt on the deal), to his great credit, said, "I'm going to drop out of this unless we're allowed to talk to customers." This led to many closed-door meetings and arguing. But finally the partners said, "Well, we've talked to Topper Toys, and they've agreed to give us ten customers to talk to."

They delegated that job to me. I dutifully called all ten customers, and sure enough, all of the customers insisted that there was a no return policy. Topper Toys looked vindicated after all. It seemed our suspicions were unfounded, and we were wrong. I'd made somewhat copious notes on each customer conversation and put them in the file. I shared the results with Conrad and our partners, and everyone basically said *Well, we tried our best. We were wrong. They were somehow able to do this. Let's go public.*

Ultimately, Topper Toys did go public, though it was a lousy stock market, and they didn't do nearly as well as they had hoped in terms of valuation. In the meantime, I had left Cogan, Berlind, Weill & Levitt to go work with another of the partners (Clarence Jones, which ultimately led to my start in media).

One day I noticed an announcement that—after going public— Topper had raised $30 million in October of '71, with Citibank representing three pension funds. Curious, I made a few calls. It turns out that Citibank hadn't done any due diligence, because Topper had just gone public. Their logic: If it had just gone public, then that round of due diligence must have been sufficient, right?

A few months later, Topper Toys went bankrupt.

In the details of their bankruptcy papers, it turns out that they were shipping roughly 42 percent of their sales to a warehouse they owned adjacent to their headquarters in Elizabeth, New Jersey. Somehow this had eluded the auditor and the due diligence process, even though we had raised substantial objections. Turns out we were right to object, but it wasn't until this disclosure that we understood exactly how they were cheating.

Immediately this triggered an SEC investigation. Soon I got a call from the law firm who was representing Topper Toys. "We just want to tell you that you're going to be a key witness, and you ought to get counsel."

Now I wasn't exactly rich at the time. "You mean, you're not going to represent me?" I asked.

"Well, no."

"Maybe I'll just go represent myself without counsel," I said, somewhat bluffing, and knowing this would really freak them out.

"Don't do that yet," the lawyer said, a bit panicked. "Let me get back to you."

Sure enough, they came back three days later and said, "Look, we'll supply you with separate counsel to represent you." And before I knew it, an SEC investigator came and deposed me.

"I'm kind of puzzled," I said to the investigator. "What's the problem here?"

"You know, Topper's whole defense is that they had a no return policy."

"Yeah, that's correct," I said, glad that we had done the due diligence and interviewed those ten customers.

"But we can't find your notes," the investigator said.

I told them the notes should be exactly where I had left them, amid all the other case files.

"We can't find them."

"Well I don't know what to tell you," I said. "There were five pages of notes for ten companies, and they were consistent in showing a no return policy."

The conversation more or less fizzled there, and it was a standoff.

I assumed this was the end of the story. But I was wrong. And to find out the rest of the tale, which happened a decade later, you'll have to read chapter 3.

TelePrompTer & Children's Television Workshop (1972–1978)

Dad's financial acumen led him to a job at TelePrompTer just a few years after he began his investment banking career. He got the job because of his ability to recognize value and opportunities that others didn't see. You can read about how that came about in chapter 2.

Then he helped run finances at the Children's Television Workshop. (You probably don't recognize the name of the company, but you'll know the name of its flagship show: *Sesame Street*.)

HBO (1978–1984)

JANE

In 1978, Dad joined HBO and only five years later became its CEO. He still hadn't turned forty. In the mid-'80s, as George Mair writes in *Inside HBO*, some thought that "Biondi had more clout in Hollywood than anyone except George Lucas." While running HBO, he helped pivot the company from a channel that distributed content to one that made it. When he arrived at HBO, it was losing money; when he left, it was making $180 million annually.

During these years, the debate in the entertainment industry gradually shifted from: *Will people be willing to pay for content?* ('60s/'70s) to *How much will people pay?* and *To whom will they be willing to pay?* (Cord cutting, the streaming wars.) This setting is important. Media companies realized that original content was king, and my father led the charge. At HBO, as George Mair writes, "Biondi taught the executives at HBO that they were not in the cable television business, they were in the entertainment business."

When building HBO from a niche distributor of boxing matches to its role as a dominant player in TV, for example, my father deployed a competitive advantage: He harnessed data that others ignored— the capital improvement plans of the cable distributors—to better understand HBO's own potential growth. This was sound research that others just didn't think of or bother to do. And it gave HBO a leg-up when negotiating with the studios for the blockbuster films that would run on the channel for years.

Coca-Cola Goes to the Movies (1985–1987)

JANE

My father is best known for running HBO, Viacom, and then Universal Studios, but in the '80s—after leading HBO—he ran the now-forgotten entertainment division of Coca-Cola.

What's that? You don't remember Coca-Cola producing movies and TV shows? You're not alone. However, in the mid-1980s, Coke realized that it had a saturated market (everybody was already drinking Coke) and venturing into the entertainment industry was one of the ways it attempted to diversify . . . and they hired my father to lead the effort. Though the fact that Coke made movies is now a mostly forgotten footnote in history, some of the movies and TV shows are very much *not* forgotten. Dad tells, in chapter 3, the story of how Coca-Cola came to create an entertainment division, and you'll find other stories about his time there later in the book.

A Life-Changing Job Offer and the Goodbye Party That Wasn't (1987)

JANE

In the 1980s, billionaire Sumner Redstone bought Viacom, whose channel, Showtime, was the only serious rival for HBO. Sumner seemed just as swashbuckling and ubiquitous as a Mark Cuban, Richard Branson, or Elon Musk. No one doubted his smarts. "Redstone had a reputation for ruthlessness from early in his career. The brilliant son of a Boston drive-in-theatre operator and night-club impresario, he worked as a tax lawyer before getting involved in National Amusements, the business his father had founded in 1936," explains Maria Bustillos in *The New Yorker*. "By the late nineteen-seventies, he had bullied his brother and father out of the way to take full control of the company. Over the next few decades, he made a series of daring, aggressive takeover bids . . . Many of his wildest risks paid off explosively."

Not everyone believed in this kind of team empowerment. One of these "wildest risks" was acquiring Viacom, and one of the first moves he made was to tap my father to run it. And that's why, when I was a young girl, I remember *almost* moving from New York to Los Angeles. Mom and Dad had picked out my school in California. I even had the uniforms ready to wear. The flights were all set. Then Sumner called.

FRANK

In early 1987, Coke decided that all of the entertainment division's assets were on the West Coast, and all the senior executives were on Fifth Avenue in New York, so the company should transfer them to California. For a variety of reasons, my boss, Fay Vincent, couldn't make the move, and the head of Columbia Pictures, Dick Gallop, was ill and also couldn't make the move. So I was nominated to go to California, where we had assiduously bought a home in Beverly Hills and gotten the kids enrolled in school.

Throughout the year we went through a process of numerous goodbye parties, culminating in a party jointly thrown by Henry Schleiff (head of business affairs at HBO, whom I had hired) and Michael Fuchs (at the time the president of HBO, who had succeeded me when I left). The gala would be held in Henry's apartment and paid for by HBO.

A few days before the big party, I received what would become a fateful phone call from Sumner Redstone, who had just purchased control of Viacom (at the time, one of HBO's main rivals—if not the only rival—in the paid TV business), inquiring as to whether I would be interested in running Viacom as the CEO, and working with him.

It was clearly a better job than running Coca-Cola's television businesses on the West Coast. Although my family and I were locked and loaded in terms of getting ready to move to California in about eight days, I accepted the job at Viacom, which was headquartered in New York.

Which meant I was staying.

I called Henry Schleiff after I accepted the job, and a day or so before the party, to inform him that "this is somewhat awkward, but we aren't going ahead with the move."

Henry, on the one hand, was thrilled for me, but he also realized the complications of a party in New York City that was being catered by Brennan's (from New Orleans), and he knew that his co-host, Michael Fuchs, needed to be told. Henry decided that it would be better for him—and not me—to tell Michael. So the day before the party, as Michael was returning from California, Henry called to tell him the "good news."

Michael was quite surprised and taken aback. His initial reaction was to cancel the party, but Henry prevailed and said we should go on with it. It happened to be an incredibly warm day in New York when we held the party, with 150 people jammed into Henry's two-bedroom apartment, and as fate would have it, the air-conditioning broke. The New Orleans chef, for some reason, needed to boil the shrimp in the bathtub.

But we turned it into a sort of "Welcome Back, Glad You're Staying!" party for all involved . . . with the possible exception of Michael, who was not at all thrilled with the prospects of me running one of their main competitors.

The Viacom Years (1987–1996)

As a result of the job offer he'd just gotten, in 1987 my father began his role as CEO of Viacom, which was, at the time, a relatively unknown media company with a mix of cable systems, radio stations, and cable channels. As Viacom grew, Dad was at one point in charge of a sprawling organization of more than 150,000 employees.

When he was the head of Viacom, my father helped MTV and Nickelodeon unlock new value from original content, ranging from

The Real World to *Rugrats*, and *Rugrats* even landed him an Emmy. He was always a believer in the power of content and consumers' demand for it. Tom Freston (then the head of MTV, which was part of Viacom) recalls some of the cutting-edge original content they developed at Viacom.

"Remember *Beavis and Butt-Head*? Frank loved that," said Tom. "We found this guy Mike Judge—who has become so influential—but we found him when he was still a hippie in Austin, doing *Beavis and Butt-Head*. I said to Frank, 'We're gonna buy this, and we'll own the IP.' Now Frank was this straight-looking guy, with the Ivy League patina, and *Beavis and Butt-Head* wasn't exactly up his alley. But he knew immediately—within seconds—that this was a great idea for MTV, and of course it went on to become a hit."

Tom continues: "Rather than licensing music videos from record companies, we actually owned this. We found young creators early on, and tried to get their early projects, and these people would go on to bigger and better things. That happened with Mike Judge, Judd Apatow, Ben Stiller, Jon Stewart."

In fact, it's tough to overstate just how dominant Viacom was at its peak. In a 1995 cover story for *Wired*, John Batelle wrote, "Look at Viacom's record. In the past 10 years, while most of the media world served up more inane sitcoms, formulaic movies, and predictable newscasts, Viacom was making MTV into the most profitable network on the globe. It was branding kids from age 3 (Nickelodeon) to age 40 (VH-1). While the big three networks thrashed about, wondering why ad revenues were falling, Viacom was buying stakes in every hot media property on cable. Now, as the kids who grew up with MTV and videogames enter their 20s, Viacom's investments are paying off." The magazine's cover image? A hilarious drawing of *Beavis and Butt-Head*, but with the faces of Sumner Redstone (as Beavis) and my father (as Butt-Head). The article's title was a nod to Beavis himself: "Viacom Doesn't Suck."

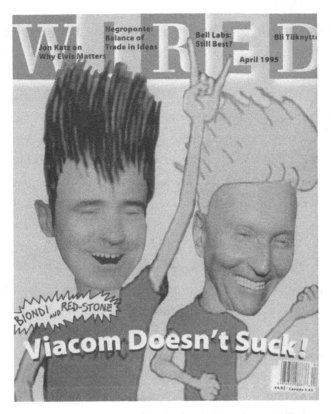

Sumner Redstone (Beavis-R) and my father (Butt-Head-L), on the cover of *Wired*.

Why I Turned Down *Lord of the Rings*: Universal Studios (1996–1998)

Dad was fired from Viacom by Sumner Redstone in 1996, a story told in chapter 7. After that, he went to work for Universal. As demonstrated by this story, Dad's attention to detail and preparation meant that more often than not his calls were excellent, but he had the humility and self-awareness to accept that you won't get it right every single time. He knew you must learn from your mistakes and move on to the next opportunity. Here's a classic story from his time at Universal Studios.

For the most part, my job was not to make creative decisions. Even as the head of a studio—at Viacom and Universal—I was simply viewed, correctly, as a businessman, and we had people working for me who made the decisions on the movies, the cast, and the stories.

Sometimes I weighed in. At times we would need to kill projects that had, somehow, worked their way up through the creative structure of the studio, and it was pretty clear that the costs were far higher than had been represented. For example, at Universal, for years we pushed back *The Hulk*, because the costs were just too high. (This ultimately worked to the benefit of the movie, as the CGI improved while the movie was delayed.)

And then there are the higher-profile pitches.

When I was running Universal in the late '90s, a young indie-director came to us with a pitch. The director didn't have many credits to his name—just a few low-budget films like *Heavenly Creatures*, about a teenage girl who murders her mother.

The director's name was Peter Jackson. And he pitched us *The Lord of the Rings*.

Universal owned the rights to *Lord of the Rings*. And Peter Jackson wanted to make it. He was banging on the Universal creative people to give him a shot.

Our creative executives were nervous, as the movies would have a price tag of $300 to $500 million, and, so far, Jackson had only worked in the art house.

But, of course, we were intrigued by the massive potential of *Lord of the Rings*, so even though it seemed risky, we didn't dismiss the idea out of hand. We said, "How about we date before we get married?"

"What do you mean?" Peter Jackson said.

"Let's make a movie with each other, with a smaller budget, but bigger than what you had been making, and see how it goes."

He agreed to the suggestion, so we signed on Michael J. Fox to *The Frighteners*. And this was a silly ghost movie that died the first weekend.

The creatives at Universal were so disappointed, they actually said, "We could never do it with him. Let's sell the rights to *Lord of the Rings* to someone who will actually make it."

So that's what we did. We sold the rights to Miramax—a part cash-sale, part trade—and we received half of *Shakespeare in Love*. This turned out to be a profitable picture, but nowhere near as lucrative as *Lord of the Rings*, of course. (One silver lining: *Shakespeare in Love* won the Academy Award for Best Picture, and since we were the domestic distributors, we received an Oscar.)

But this kind of thing happens. You're making decisions on people you don't know and you haven't really worked with, and they might have just happened to have a bad day or a good day.

A July 11, 1997, photo of my father with his CEO peers featured in *Vanity Fair*, October 1997.

Back row, left to right: Berkshire Hathaway chairman Warren Buffett, Universal chairman Frank Biondi, Time Warner president Richard Parsons, TCI chairman John Malone, NBC president Bob Wright, Sony's Howard Stringer, Seagram president Edgar Bronfman Jr., Universal president Ron Meyer, Intel chairman Andrew Grove, Warner Bros. chairman Terry Semel, Comcast's Ralph Roberts, News Corp.'s Rupert Murdoch. Center row: Microsoft's Nathan Myhrvold, Time Warner chairman Gerald Levin, Orca Bay Capital Corp. chairman John McCaw Jr., ICM's Jeff Berg, DreamWorks partner David Geffen, *Washington Post* company chairwoman Katharine Graham, Microsoft chairman Bill Gates. Front row: Herbert A. Allen of Allen & Co., Sony president Nobuyuki Idei, HSN chairman Barry Diller, Dream Works partner Jeffrey Katzenberg.

The Final Chapter (1998–2019)

JANE

After Dad left Universal, he spent more than a decade running an investment fund named WaterView, which is a classic good luck/ bad timing story you'll read about in chapter 9. He and his partners had a number of failures but one huge success, The Tennis Channel.

Dad never officially retired and was still serving on multiple boards on the day he died—including the board of Madison Square Garden, the irony of which will become clearer in chapter 8.

For the rest of this book, you'll read more about the principle my father used during his remarkable career that allowed him to seize his destiny in moving from a lucky high school student to one of the most respected (though unheralded) figures in the entertainment industry. Hope you enjoy the ride!

CHAPTER 2

Live with Integrity

"Whatever you choose to do, do it with integrity," my father once said in a commencement speech to the graduates of Claremont University's Graduate School of Business. "It is the most valuable asset that you bring to a career and ultimately leave with. In the end, it is the ultimate insurance that you will never have to look back with regret."

My father treated people how he (or anyone, really) would want to be treated. He was respectful, always, even to those who didn't return the favor.

The stories in this chapter speak to my father's unwavering sense of fairness and how that paid dividends both for him and the shareholders. In the early days of cable, for example, the nascent industry was one that not a lot of people understood, so some in power took advantage of that confusion with sketchy practices . . . such as sloppy, misleading accounting. In the story "Accounting for the Footnotes" (p. 30), my father refused to cut these kinds of corners and blew the whistle on an accounting problem that threatened to decimate the entire industry.

My father's decency and integrity were what distinguished him, and these are the qualities that his family, friends, and colleagues spoke about most when memorializing him after he died. Living with integrity is a choice, and it's one that's worth the effort.

Accounting for the Footnotes

JANE

As we see in this story, sometimes you don't even know what the right thing is until you've rolled up your sleeves and dug in to learn.

FRANK

In late 1971, just three years into my investment banking career, I had been working for a man named Clarence Jones, an African American investment banker. Clarence was once a partner of a top securities firm, CBWL-Hayden, Stone, and now he wanted to hang his own shingle and start the nation's first Black media company. I thought that was a great idea. I worked with Clarence to help start the company, but it turns out that he couldn't raise the money, and he couldn't afford to pay me. At the time I was in my twenties. I lived with a roommate in a small apartment on 62nd Street and couldn't exactly afford to work pro bono.

While Clarence could no longer pay me a salary, he gave me the next best thing—a connection. His wife worked for the largest cable company in the country at the time, TelePrompTer, which was a real media darling. "They're looking for financial executives," he told me. "Interested?"

"Sure."

My first interview was with a lawyer who, I hoped, would give me a fair shake thanks to Clarence's glowing endorsement.

The lawyer looked at me. "You realize Clarence's recommendation of a financial executive I view as equivalent to *my* recommendation for brain surgeons. And I'm a lawyer. And my four brothers are all rabbis."

The interview was off to a great start. Later in the conversation, the lawyer told me that the firm's senior executives were desperately trying to sell the company (TelePrompTer) because the current owner, Jack Kent Cooke, better known as the owner of the Washington

Redskins, had had a massive heart attack, and no one believed he would survive. So while Cooke recuperated in the hospital, the other executives shopped the firm to deep-pocketed companies like Xerox and IBM, hoping for a high multiple on earnings.

"Well, have you tried Western Union?" I asked.

He just gave me a look, maybe mildly interested. "No," he said. "Tell me about it."

I gave him a thumbnail description of Western Union, or at least what I knew. I had done my homework and knew the industry well. No one thinks of Western Union as a growth company—they were founded before the Civil War!—but at the time, the stock sold for a large multiple (a high price to earnings ratio), and it could be a potential buyer.

The lawyer considered all of this. He had a good poker face.

"Look. I like you," he said. "Call me in a week. I want to follow this up."

The man was good to his word. A week later we spoke and he said, "The Western Union idea was a dead end, but I like the way you were thinking. I've got a proposal for you. Would you do a one-year consultancy? I want you to value TelePrompTer, based on public information only."

Hmmm. A one-year consultancy, while potentially interesting, didn't have the same security as a full-time job.

Then I found out they would triple my old salary.

Naturally, I immediately got to work. My job was to scour all of the available data and then give a logical, objective, clear-eyed assessment of what the company was worth. For the 99.9 percent of the world that's not in the investment banking community, that's a big part of what they do: estimate value. You take a look at how much money the company made (or lost) in the past, how much they're making now, and how much they're likely to make in the future. You factor in the risk, often with discount rates. You make some assumptions about growth. You look at other similar companies to do some benchmarking. As you'll see in many other stories in this book, estimating value was the meat-and-potatoes work I'd do for the next thirty-plus years, whether as a junior consultant or running HBO or Viacom.

My office at TelePrompTer didn't have a computer. Using an HP-80 Hewlett-Packard calculator and lined sheets of paper, we did all of the math by hand. And how did we find our research? For this, we had to rely upon what the lawyer had said, "public information only," meaning the financial statements and prospectuses that had been publicly disclosed. These days people think of cable companies as stodgy old dinosaurs, but in the '70s, they were the high-tech darlings. This was the start of the cable boom. Most of the key companies had either gone public or raised extensive capital, and whenever you do that, you need to file paperwork. We tracked down all of that paperwork and we analyzed it.

"I don't want you to rush," he had said, so I had the luxury of spending the year figuring out how and why cable companies made money. The return on assets, the return on equity, the leverage ratios—I learned all of these in great detail. I really got to know the statistics of the cable industry, probably as well as anybody working in the area at that time.

At the end of the year I presented my analysis to the lawyer, who said, "I like this stuff. Why don't you come work for us? You can do mergers and acquisitions, you can do Wall Street relationships, and you can do budgeting for the company."

And just like that, I had officially started my first full-time job in the media industry. It was going well, and one night I got a call again from the lawyer, who said, "What are you doing tomorrow?"

"Well, what *should* I be doing tomorrow?"

He told me to head up to the 34th floor of the Time Inc. building, where I'd meet with the assistant treasurer for non-magazine affairs, a man (amazingly) named Nicholas Nicholas. It turns out that Tele-PrompTer wanted to buy a division of Time Inc.—Southern Manhattan Cable—and my job, as usual, was to pore through the paperwork and do a valuation, comparing it to the value of TelePrompTer. You probably haven't heard of Manhattan Cable, but I bet you're familiar with one of their prized assets: Home Box Office. (This same Nicholas would later be my boss at HBO—the world of media is a small place.)

Something about the numbers didn't quite add up. Ironically, the two franchises were almost identical in size and subscribers, and the rates were identical, but we (at TelePrompTer) were able to report a profit of over a million dollars, while Time (owner of HBO) was losing over a million dollars a year, and they were ready to throw in the towel.

"We can't figure out how you guys are making money, and we're losing money," said Nick, my eventual boss.

"Well, look, why don't you give me a copy of your last year's financials, as a starting point?" I asked him.

I dug through the financials, and the income statement was in a format I had never seen. Like most income statements, it had the usual categories like revenues, debt expenses, and net revenues. But on the expenses side, under the marketing expenses, it had a line that said "Capitalized Property Plant and Equipment."

They were using something called "utility accounting," where when you construct a grid or a system, you're allowed to capitalize certain direct and indirect construction costs as an asset, so you can recover it over the life of the plant.

(Stay with me here.) So I looked at this financial statement from Manhattan Cable (HBO), and then I called up our controller from TelePrompTer, and I told him, "I've got these income statements from Manhattan Cable, and they're in a format I've never seen before. Can you come take a look?"

The controller examined the financials.

"Are we doing the same thing?" I asked him, meaning, are we using the same form of utility accounting?

"Sure," he said. "Give me twenty-four hours, and I'll reproduce our income statement in this same format."

So he did. And when you looked at these two income statements in the same apples-to-apples format, many of the numbers were very similar: revenue (in the ballpark of $30 million for each system), and then expenses *pre-capitalization*. Yet one thing was very different: We (TelePrompTer) showed $1 million profit, and Manhattan Cable showed a $1 million loss.

I quickly had a suspicion of what caused this discrepancy. "So what's the theory here?" I asked our controller, basically knowing the answer but wanting to hear him say it.

"Oh, you know, during construction, you're allowed to capitalize all these direct and indirect costs," he said, explaining that we (Tele-PrompTer) decided to capitalize something like $7 million of costs per year, and Time Inc. (HBO) only capitalized $3 or $4 million per year. In other words, when we reclassified an expense as a capital asset, that made our costs lower and our profits higher. Or, to be more blunt, the only difference between these two companies, essentially, was an accounting decision—how much to capitalize.

"Okay, I get it," I said to the controller. "But what happens when we stop construction?"

"Well, then you have to start expensing all of these costs."

We talked through some more line items and expenses, and I eventually said, "So that means that if we stopped construction, we're just going to start losing money hand over fist?"

He just kind of shook his head and said, "Well, I guess you're right, yeah."

At that point I looked at him and said, "Do we do this anywhere else at the company?"

He explained that they didn't do this anywhere else on a system level, but at the end of each quarter, he and his counterpart (another assistant controller at the parent company) made a journal entry to capitalize a certain amount of construction costs to property, plant, and equipment.

"How much are we talking about, in terms of the size of that journal entry?" I asked.

He said $7 million, $8 million, or $9 million a quarter.

"So we're capitalizing $35, $36 million per year?"

"Yeah, rough justice."

To put this in perspective: The company had $72 million in revenue and $16 million in pretax income, so the fact that we were capitalizing some $30-plus million and not disclosing it was, to say the least, pretty relevant information. Technically, there was some *partial* disclosure: a footnote to the prior year's financial statements said something like, "We capitalize some direct costs related to construction and interest expense of $3.2 million per year," and the way it was written gives you the impression that $3.2 million was the largest number capitalized, because it's the only number cited. Meanwhile, there was another $33 million being capitalized and not disclosed.

Long story short? This was a very big deal. And now I was in an interesting position, as I had knowledge that could undo the entire company.

I didn't view my next decision as a hard call. There really was no choice: this had to be disclosed. This couldn't be buried. I immediately took it to my boss, our chief financial officer, who was brand new at the job—he hadn't even moved his family from Pittsburgh—and the senior controller, who had been there about a year.

"Hey guys, let me explain something I just learned," I told them, and then walked through the problem.

Their eyeballs almost popped out. *It couldn't be, it couldn't be,* they kept saying.

"I'm afraid it is."

Everybody was stunned.

After poring through the numbers with my bosses, we were concerned that there was something pretty close to fraud going on here. And we were suddenly in the middle of it.

Now at the same time, we were about to get listed on the New York Stock Exchange. And the NYSE has an application form, called a "listing document," that has to be signed by the chief accounting officer.

My revelation bubbled up right in the middle of this NYSE listing. On the one hand, our financials had been signed off by an outside auditor before I dropped the bombshell. Yet even with the auditor's blessing, our new controller said, to his credit, "I'm not going to sign it. It's not accurate."

The response by his bosses? *Either sign this or you're fired.*

The controller refused.

Just as the axe was about to fall on the controller, the auditor called and effectively said, "We're pulling our certification on these financials. We agree there's a lack of disclosure here."

There was a lot of mumbling from our superiors. They finally concluded, "We'll change the language on the NYSE disclosure. And no one's going to read this listing document, so it won't make any difference." So they changed the language, they signed the document, and TelePrompTer was listed on the New York Stock Exchange.

But our CFO decided that it was time to engage an outside lawyer, so he met with a lawyer named Bill Williams at Sullivan & Cromwell, who had just successfully finished a trial involving Penn Central and the SEC. The lawyer invited us (including me) to have dinner and fill him in.

At the restaurant we gave him the whole story, and he looked at us and said, "You've got a problem. There's a disclosure issue here, and it's serious." (I wasn't an officer of the company, so I wouldn't have any personal liability, but the CFO and the controller could be in hot water.)

It turned out that Bill Williams couldn't represent us. Because of his just-completed case with Penn Central and the SEC, he was now somewhat notorious in the regulation circles, and as he put it, "When I walk into the SEC these days, alarm bells go off. You just won't get a fair hearing."

So instead, Bill had us work with another lawyer, who said he would call the SEC and use fake names—as a hypothetical—and explain the situation for the Commission, just to get their reaction.

The lawyer called the SEC using made-up names from a made-up company, kind of like how you would say, "My *friend* has a question," when clearly you're asking for yourself. Twenty minutes later the lawyer called us back and said, "You're not going to believe this. They guessed who it was."

So the SEC now knew of the TelePrompTer shenanigans. And at this point, everything began to hit the fan. The SEC started an investigation—both into TelePrompTer and into the larger cable industry.[1] They suspended the stock from trading for one hundred days.

And in the offices of TelePrompTer, morale collapsed. The stock had traded in the $40s, and now it was below $1. There were massive layoffs. The finance department, interestingly, was one of the few groups that did *not* get fired, as we were still furnishing numbers for the SEC investigation. The bosses at TelePrompTer, I'm guessing, were afraid the SEC would have frowned upon them canning us.

As details emerged from the SEC investigation, it became somewhat apparent that most, if not all, of the cable industry used the same kind of accounting with the same kind of disclosure, or lack of disclosure. The stock prices for the entire industry cratered. The industry took a tailspin that took years to recover from.

The moral of the story? Always pay attention to the footnotes.*

JANE

*There's actually one more footnote to this story that my father didn't mention. In an unrelated matter, my father believed it was too expensive for TelePrompTer to keep adding local cable franchises. So one night, when he was working late, he shared his thoughts on the P&L with

---

1   "Fraud Suit Charges Teleprompter, Still Under a Suspension," *New York Times*, September 27, 1973, p. 67.

the employee working on these franchise applications. The employee was a woman named Carol. Their conversation lasted longer than expected, so afterward they went out for burgers. They never went on a date with anyone else for the rest of their lives, and of course I would later know Carol as just Mom.

Yahoo! Board of Directors

JANE

Long before "google" became a verb, Yahoo! was the undisputed internet search leader. They enjoyed so much market share and controlled such a large swath of the internet that they began to adopt a cavalier attitude. Yahoo! never adequately dealt with the Google challenge. They let the opportunity to become bigger slip away through a combination of arrogance and some managers who showed a lack of integrity, which my father witnessed during his time on their board of directors.

FRANK

Late in the first decade of the 2000s, I joined the Yahoo! board as a member, designated by Carl Icahn, who had been threatening to wage a proxy fight with the company in order to push through a sale to Microsoft.[2,3] I had to give up the Bank of New York board to do so, but I really thought Yahoo! still had some gas left in its tank and that I had something to add.

But after getting to the board, it was apparent that the company was somewhat leaderless.[4] There was indecision as to who should be running the company and what kind of executive should be

---

2   Yi-Wyn Yen, "Yahoo in Faceoff with Icahn," *CNN*, May 15, 2008, https://money.cnn.com/2008/05/15/technology/yahoo_icahn.fortune/index.htm?postversion=2008051520.

3   Michele Gershberg, Tiffany Wu, "Yahoo and Icahn Settle, Microsoft Deal Seen Adrift," *Reuters*, July 21, 2008, https://www.reuters.com/article/us-yahoo-icahn/yahoo-and-icahn-settle-microsoft-deal-seen-adrift-idUSDIS14163720080721.

4   Stefanie Olsen, "Will Yahoo's Board Also Get a Makeover?," *CNET*, June 22, 2007, https://www.cnet.com/tech/tech-industry/will-yahoos-board-also-get-a-makeover/.

running the company. It was publicly known that there were factions on the board.

Over the course of several months, it became apparent that Yahoo!, which possessed the search business, was undecided, internally, about the Microsoft deal.

In the process we searched for a CEO and ultimately decided on hiring Carol Bartz, who had a stellar reputation in the tech industry. She came to Yahoo! to try and deal with the confusion and the lack of unanimity—among the management and the board—about the future of the company.[5]

She did a fine job in doing the financial analysis that indicated that staying in the search business was not something Yahoo! could afford if they wanted to seriously compete with Google. The process of going back and forth about the decision dragged on for nearly two years, and the company was getting nowhere. There was no new revenue growth. Many of the initiatives did not prove fruitful.

At the end of the second year, in February, we had an executive session that had something of a freeform conversation. A few of the directors said to Carol and Jerry Yang, in particular, that we needed to pursue more acquisitions and that there was not nearly enough activity on that front.

Jerry took that a little personally. "Well listen," he began, and named off several potential acquisition candidates they had met with over the Christmas holidays. "We really haven't been able to get anything to come to fruition."

To honor the exclusivity of the executive session, I will not name the longtime Yahoo! director whom I was sitting next to and who was kind of like, "What? What are you talking about? I never heard about any of these meetings."

There was a very good case that, ostensibly, his committee should

5   Erick Schonfeld, "Bartz Calls Yahoo's Board a Bunch of 'Doofuses,'" *TechCrunch*, September 8, 2011, https://techcrunch.com/2011/09/08/bartz-calls-yahoo-board-doofuses/.

have been heavily involved in any conversations that might have led to an acquisition. Jerry realized that he had put his proverbial foot in his mouth, and he reacted by saying, "Listen, it's about time you all realize that the management here has had to dumb down almost every conversation for this board."

Silence. A caterpillar could have been heard crawling across the rug. People were in shock. And after that, the longtime director decided it was time to end his relationship with the company and resigned.

I guess it was that kind of behavior, corporate governance, and leadership that led to Yahoo! losing its internet search dominance.

Integrity in Everyday Life

JANE

Part of Dad's definition of integrity was to do the right thing whether or not anyone was watching. This played out in every aspect of his life, whether at work or play.

For example, tennis was one of Dad's great passions (more on this later in the book). A frequent partner of his, Phil McGraw (Dr. Phil), describes how Dad's integrity shone through even on the tennis courts. "I embrace the definition of integrity that most people do—doing the right thing when nobody's watching. And that's Frank," says Dr. Phil.

He elaborates on why this is more important than you'd think. "Plato once said that you can learn more about a man in an hour of play than a year of conversation. I think that's one of the things that best describes Frank Biondi," Dr. Phil says. He remembers my father as fiercely competitive on the courts, and how "he'll fight to the death on a weekend match." But at the same time, if his opponent's ball touches the line, "If it's 99.9 percent out, to him, it's 100 percent in. It doesn't matter if he needs that point more than anything in the world. He's straight up. You never had to worry about Frank. He'll fight you hard, but then he'd beat you fair."

While it's rewarding to have others affirm that Dad was honest in every aspect of his life, it was his integrity in business dealings that allowed him to have such a successful and rewarding career. Martin Shafer, co-founder and CEO of Castle Rock, views my father as an example of how it's possible to live with integrity—and decency—even in industries that aren't known for it.

"You can be a nice guy, an honest guy, a decent person, and also be successful in the movie business. It's not mutually exclusive," says Martin. "You don't have to be a stereotypical studio head-guy. You can win in this business by being honest and reasonable, and dealing with people in a forthright way."

Sherry Lansing, the former chairman and CEO of Paramount Pictures who ran the studio after it was acquired by Viacom, worked for my father at Viacom, and later served with him on several boards. "Frank was the moral compass," she recalls. "I always knew that he would never let a company do anything tricky, or funny, or put any of us at risk. He was brilliant with the numbers, and equally brilliant in understanding the business . . . and understanding people. He had great integrity, great ethics."

There are countless others in the industry—including CEOs, titans of media—who have said something similar. "I know a little bit about the executive life in this industry, and Frank was truly unique. In a world dominated by egos and self-aggrandizement, Frank was the one outlier," says Peter Chernin, who worked for my father in the mid-'80s at Showtime, before running News Corp and then founding Chernin Entertainment, which produced hit films like *Hidden Figures* and *Ford v Ferrari*. "He was never puffed up and impressed with himself. He never looked to take credit for everything. And he certainly never looked to climb over others for his own success."

Success can be slippery and squishy, but integrity is the one bedrock. "I'm old enough and sober enough to know how transitory success is in the industry. It truly means nothing," Peter Chernin goes on to say. "What does mean everything is character—how you treat people, how you conduct yourself, what you stand for. On the test of character and decency, Frank is at the absolute pinnacle of everyone I've worked with in Hollywood. And at the end of the day, that's the real mark of a life well lived."

CHAPTER 3

Do the Work

JANE It can seem like the mega success stories in business—or any field—
are fueled by extraordinary talent or unique skills. That gives the
false impression that if we want to rise to the top, then we need to be
some kind of revolutionary genius like Steve Jobs or Elon Musk. Yet
greatness doesn't require any special "CEO gene."

The small things matter. When you do the small things well, over
time, that can have a compounding effect. A core theme to my father's
success was mastering all of the things that are in your control: staying
curious, constantly learning, showing up (on time), and following
through on your commitments. Doing the work.

He was always interested in understanding how things worked.
"I've always believed you have to really understand your industry,"
he once said. "I know that sounds so obvious, but it's amazing to me
how many people don't really have that much depth of knowledge in
the business they're in." He fed his curiosity and continued to learn
by reading—a lot. He read everything.

"Frank was extremely well-read. I don't mean only in terms of
novels and biographies, but he just read every periodical in the world,"
remembers Henry Schleiff, his longtime colleague and friend. Henry
worked for my father at both HBO and Viacom, and later he ran the
Hallmark channel.

"Over the weekend, I would try to read every goddamn thing I could, every trade publication, *Variety*, *Hollywood Reporter*, journals about the business, and of course the Sunday *[New York] Times* cover to cover," says Henry, "because I'd get in there on Monday morning, and Frank would say, 'Did you see that article on? . . . ' It reached the point where he said, 'You know, there was an article in *Field and Stream*.' It was impossible to keep up. He was just voracious in his knowledge."

My father loved to just *do the work*, no matter how unglamorous, no matter if it might seem boring to most. He didn't cut corners. He prided himself on understanding his industry and competitors. "There's just a wealth of resources on your competition in the press, on television, in symposiums, and in industry gatherings. It's out there," Dad said. "It's like solving a puzzle, and you can connect the dots if you do enough of it."

He would often quote Stephen Hawking, "Half the battle is just showing up." *Keep at things*, he would implore, especially when they are tough. He taught me this with both words and examples. When I needed to run an eight-minute mile to make the high school tennis team, he ran with me weekend after weekend, up hill after hill, until I cracked the eight-minute mark.

Dad was a master of the tiny details. When you dig in to understand the granularity, you find surprising opportunities that others may have overlooked.

This is what my father did at Coca-Cola in the 1980s. Thanks to his grasp of the finer points of discount rates—a level of expertise that even his CFO lacked—he had the confidence to propose an aggressive acquisition. Because he did more homework than anyone else in the room, his persuasion had real power. Those tiny details would later translate into blockbuster headlines and massive value.

There are more ways to change the status quo than being loud, brash, or flamboyant. If you need your boss to take a chance on a great idea? Master the minutiae, and you'll show them how it can be done.

Facts Are Everything

JANE

This story is just a small vignette, but it says a ton about the contrast between how my father viewed the world and how others could take a more loosey-goosey approach to "facts." And in our modern era where the truth seems up for debate—with even basic facts disputed by many—it can pay to have more vigilance about what's real and what's conjecture.

FRANK

Billionaire Sumner Redstone, owner of Viacom, where I worked from 1987 to 1996, loved to write his own speeches, which were curiously effective but took a long time for him to craft. On one plane trip, he said to me, "Listen to this. Simon & Schuster has a 25 percent share of the book market in the People's Republic of China."

I just looked at him and laughed and said, "Well, that's not true."

He looked at me. "How do you know?"

"Because it's a fact," I said.

Sumner looked at me again and then quickly grabbed the phone off the wall of the airplane. He started punching in a phone number, calling the PR person who was helping him with his speech, and he started yammering about Simon & Schuster's market share in China.

About three hours later he received a phone call. He looked at me with his wry smile, and he said, "Try this on for size. Simon & Schuster has a 25 percent share of the *English language* book market in the People's Republic of China."

I just laughed and said, "I'm not sure that's true, but it's certainly a much more reasonable guess than the first one."

Broken Toys, Part 2: The Little Details with Big Impact

JANE

In Part 1 of this story from chapter 1, we learned that Topper Toys tried to hide its unprofitability by doing a runaround with their "no return policy" (by shipping excess inventory to a warehouse). That led to a federal investigation and a lawsuit.[6] Dad picks up the story about a decade later, long after Topper Toys went bankrupt, and once again shows how his mastery of tiny details was invaluable to the companies he worked for.

About a decade after my experience with Topper Toys' accounting games and their deceiving "no return policy," I got another call from the law firm representing Topper Toys, who said that the firm had moved to some new offices downtown. In the process of the move, they found my old files and the notes I had taken with the ten Topper Toys customers when I talked to them about that no return policy.

At about the same time as I got this call, I had heard from friends who worked at the SEC that the law firm was trying to pin the blame on me, as I was the most junior guy on the totem pole.

"We're going to come back up and re-depose you," they said.

As a result, years after the original conversation, we went back through my dusty old notes. And the notes were relatively consistent. But one of the things they also asked in the original deposition: *Did you recommend underwriters insurance to Topper?*

"Yes, we did recommend underwriters insurance," I told the SEC. "Topper asked us to get a quote, and we did, and they said, 'No thank you, it's too expensive. We have general liability insurance.'"

The SEC guy—the one doing the deposition—said "okay" and noted that in the records.

Soon I received another call from the law firm, saying, "Hey, we're going to trial. You're going to be one of the key witnesses." *Great.* And the lawsuit now had staggering financial implications, as millions were at stake.

They asked me to come down to their firm near Wall Street, located at the sixty-story skyscraper One Chase Manhattan Plaza, to prepare

6   "Complaint Names Topper Corp., Others," *SEC News Digest*, Issue 73-719 (SEC Docket, Vol. 5, No. 2–Nov. 27), November 13, 1973, p. 1.

for the trial. I took an elevator up to one of the highest floors. They escorted me to a dark conference room.

A few lawyers sat in the dark room. They introduced me to a new partner, and he was speculating how the case might play out, when the senior partner burst into the room and said, "Goddamnit!" We all looked at him. The senior partner continued shouting about why the case was going to trial, bemoaning that there was no insurance to settle.

"Excuse me," I piped in. "Who told you that?"

The lawyer opened up my deposition, and it was a *long* deposition, so he thumbed through the paperwork for an uncomfortable amount of time. He finally found the page and read from the document: *Did you recommend underwriters insurance? Yes. The company asked for a quote. They didn't like the quote, they turned it down.*

"That's underwriters insurance," I said. "They turned it down because they have general liability policies!"

The distinction, of course, was subtle but quite material: Topper had declined *underwriting* insurance, which was relevant when they prepared to go public. But this dispute was clearly covered by *general liability* insurance. Once again, the tiny details matter, and often they're not as tiny as they seem.

And soon, one of the era's largest legal cases was settled.[7]

The Devil Is in the Discount Rate: Why Coca-Cola Bought Embassy Pictures

For a brief period in the 1980s, Coca-Cola was in the movie business. The reason? They had done some market research and discovered some good news and bad news. The good news: Everyone's drinking Coke. The bad news: Everyone's drinking Coke. They worried that if they only stuck to soda, they could only grow as fast as the per-capita birth rate.

---

7 "Orenstein, Others, Enjoined," *SEC News Digest*, Issue 74-54 (SEC Docket, Vol. 3, No. 20–Apr. 2), March 19, 1974, p. 2.

Coke needed to diversify. So they looked around for possible industries to invest in, and they narrowed it down to the entertainment business and pharmaceuticals. They flirted with going into pharma but finally rejected the idea because of all the government regulation.

First, Coke purchased Columbia Pictures. Then they wanted to get bigger. The easiest way to do that, of course, is to acquire movie and TV companies, and in 1985, after my stint running HBO, I was hired to do just that.

The entirety of my "division" was one analyst, one assistant, and me. That was it. We worked out of Coca-Cola's New York headquarters at 5th Avenue and 55th Street, and our floor was filled with antique colonial furniture, Coca-Cola paraphernalia, and zero people.

Where do you look to find possible acquisitions? It helps to know people. The investment banking world is pretty small—and the movie/TV slice of investment banking is even smaller—so if you keep good personal relationships, you'll have a feel for the companies in play. Through my relationship with Jerry Perenchio (a future billionaire who later owned Univision), I knew he was part of a movie and TV company that he and his partner, Norman Lear, were trying to sell: Embassy.

You probably haven't heard the name Embassy, but I bet you've heard of their work—movies like *The Graduate*, *The Producers* (the original one), *Escape from New York*, and *This Is Spinal Tap*. They also cranked out TV hits like *The Jeffersons*, *The Facts of Life*, *Diff'rent Strokes*, and *Who's the Boss*. Especially for a company like Coca-Cola that had zero movie and TV assets to their name, Embassy was an attractive target, with a $500 million price tag.

Was it worth it?

To figure that out, my "division" pored through all of Embassy's financial statements and records. We spread all of the paperwork over the empty desks—we had plenty of them—and spent weeks punching numbers on our calculators. This was before Excel or Google Sheets.

We soon figured out that while Embassy's film division had a decorated past—*The Graduate! The Producers!*—in 1985, at least, it was losing money. But their TV shows were gold and they were making money, lots of money, as the TV stations wrote them checks each month.

How could we determine if Embassy was worth $500 million? There are several ways to estimate value. One common answer is "whatever the market will pay," but there's also a basic method that's well-known to finance types and not so obvious to the rest of the world.

Basically, you do your best to estimate all of the company's profits and losses (or cash flows) in the future, and then you convert these "future values" back to how much they're worth today, using a discount rate. The higher the risk you face, the larger the discount rate, and the less something is worth today.

Say you expect to receive $100 five years from today. If it's a rock solid treasury bond, the discount rate might be 3 percent, meaning the $100 payoff would be worth $84 today. That is, it would be a smart decision to invest $84 today because you're pretty sure you'll get $100 five years from now.

On the other hand, if it's a risky tech start-up, the discount rate could be as high as 20 percent, and that $100 payoff is only worth about $40 today. An investor wants a bigger discount rate on risky investments because they are less certain they will reap the reward.

In short, higher risk = less certainty = lower value of the investment today = a higher discount rate.

I know, I know . . . most of you didn't mean to buy a finance textbook—and those of you who did, please see the appendix where I show the equation I used to determine the present and future values. But bear with me. The fact that this stuff can be dry and confusing is why people lose money. It pays to stick with it. What a company's future value is worth today is an arcane-sounding question. I wouldn't lead with that at a cocktail party. Questions like "*What's the most appropriate discount rate?*" are far too dry to fetch headlines or break into the mainstream, but in my experience, it's a solid understanding of these technicalities—even though there's no sizzle, no glamour, no cameras—that can flip the fortunes of a company.

Think of your favorite movie. Think of your favorite show. Whether they get made at all, and who makes them, can hinge on what might seem, to many, a tedious financial footnote indicating what discount rate was used to estimate the current value of an investment that will pay off in the future. That is, the decision the studio and all the parties make about investing in a particular movie or TV series depends in part on what they'd have to spend today and how much that investment would be worth in the future. (One of the reasons that I've been the CEO of HBO, Viacom, and Universal Studios is that I was willing to do the work of slogging through these kinds of boring details when others focused on the flash.)

As I was crunching all the numbers for Embassy, I called up the chief financial officer of Coca-Cola, Doug Ivester, who ultimately went on to become Coke's CEO. "Hey, Doug, what are the rules at Coke for discounting cash flows?"

"Use an after-tax discount rate of 16 percent," Doug said.

Wow. I thought about that for a second; 16 percent is awfully high.

"Really, Doug?" I asked. "That's pretty severe."

Doug was firm: 16 percent it was. This was on the extremely high side—meaning the company was attaching a lot of risk to their investments—which makes it a tough hurdle to clear. In other words, saying that you will *only* invest in projects that clear a 16 percent discount rate means that you will make fewer investments and end up with a lot of investments that have relatively low risk. It's a conservative strategy, and Coca-Cola was a conservative company. (Aside: Years later, when I ran Viacom, I tried to encourage us to take smart risks. If seven out of ten decisions are good, you're probably not taking enough chances.)

So we used Doug's rules, discounting each future cash flow back to its present value at 16 percent. As a concrete example of how much this matters: the value of $100 million five years from now has a present value of $41 million at a 16 percent discount rate; it would have a present value of $63 million if the discount rate was 8 percent.

At 16 percent, the cash flows added up to a present value of about $365 million, which was far short of the $500 million price tag.

Then I thought some more about it. I realized that most of the future cash flows—to the tune of $900 million worth—were coming *not* from speculative movies that could be blockbusters or could be duds, but rather from the more routine receivables (contractual payments) from TV stations for the sale of Embassy's shows. When Embassy sells a show like *Who's the Boss* to the TV stations, the stations are contractually bound to pay them in the future. That's not very risky.

Most of these payments were due within forty-eight months. These were practically AAA bonds, which tend to have rates like 3 percent or 4 percent. So why the heck was Coke forcing us to discount them at 16 percent? This was an example of "corporate think," where one global rule is meant to apply to every situation. It can pay to be a little more creative, even in jobs that are not considered "creative."

I called our CFO back.

"Doug, I've got a question for you. I can send my ten-year-old daughter to the bank, and they would give her $900 million for these receivables if discounted at 4 percent. Why are you forcing me to discount them at 16 percent?" I made my case: If they separated the transactions into clusters of receivables, most of them were highly secured and very creditworthy—meaning a lower discount rate would be appropriate; only a smaller subset would have some riskier futures that they would be betting on, like the movies.

"Let me think about it," said Doug.

The next day he called me back. "I've got a proposition for you. I'll let you discount the receivables at 4 percent, but everything else you've got to discount at 20 percent."

We got back to work. My entire department—me and the one analyst—broke out our trusty calculators and again ran the numbers. Lo and behold, it came out to be somewhere around the $500 million mark.

We went to Embassy, made our bid, and they accepted it. (The final deal went for around $485 million, once we adjusted for working capital and undisclosed liabilities and yada yada.)

The aftermath?

My ten-year-old daughter never needed to get involved, but we did the next best thing. One year later, Coke took these TV receivables to Citibank. The bank did the same math I did. The bank was now in my shoes: they had to estimate their value.

The bank used a discount rate not of 16 percent, or 10 percent, or 8 percent . . . they decided that these receivables were so rock solid that they used 4 percent.

The bank bought them for $1 billion.

So within twelve months, we had made Coca-Cola $500 million of pure profit. It was an enormous score.

And then I realized one additional technical detail: Thanks to Coke's acquisition of Embassy, suddenly my staff was a bit larger than one person, and now I was in charge of an entire TV company.

Know the Value of Data

JANE

Here my father pulls back the curtain to reveal a surprising driver of success at HBO, which is less about Tony Soprano and more about a clever way to use data that no one else had considered.

FRANK

What was the basis of my success at HBO in the early 1980s? How did the company become profitable?

We did one very simple thing that no other cable company was doing: We asked our customers about their construction plans.

By "customers" I don't mean the end-viewers watching movies at home, but instead the cable operators. We asked the cable operators, essentially, "What are your construction plans over the next thirty-six months?"

They were usually happy to tell us. They would say things like, "Well, I'm going to build 8,000 miles of cable, and it's going to pass through 800,000 people, and we'll get 400,000 new cable subscribers."

We had been asking that question for a while, but before I took over, the marketing team hadn't really used that data. Here's how I wanted to use it: If we knew the cable operators' growth plans, then we could better forecast the future HBO subscriber base.

In the above example, if the cable operator expected 400,000 new cable subscribers in the future, we could assume that would mean 200,000 new HBO subscribers, give or take.

Why did this data matter? It gave us a tremendous advantage when negotiating what we would pay movie studios for content, which was—at the time—the lifeblood of our programming.

The studios wanted to lock in long-term deals, with the rights spread out over many years. And they tended to sell content (movies) based on a *per-subscriber* rate. They would say, basically, "This movie is worth 50 cents a sub[scriber]." And if they forecasted us to have six million subscribers in five years, then they might sell us the rights to the movie for $3 million. They based their estimate of our future subscriber count—six million, in this example—on rudimentary growth assumptions.

But we had a better forecast. By creating our own home-grown model of growth—using the cable operators' internal construction plans—we knew what the studios didn't: our subscriber count would likely jump to ten million, not six million. And if we bought the rights to that movie (for example) for $3 million, then the per-subscriber cost plunged from 50 cents to 30 cents, a massive drop in costs and a huge boost to our profits.

Except we didn't grow to ten million subs . . . we grew to sixteen million. And thanks to this data, our programming costs plummeted on a per-subscriber basis, our profit margins surged, and we were big heroes for pulling this off. And the studios hated us.

JANE

Here my father indulged in a bit of hyperbole. The studios might have "hated" HBO for that shrewd negotiating coup, yet in a larger sense, they relied on—and possibly even loved—HBO for its newfound role in co-financing new films. As George Mair writes in *Inside HBO*, thanks to my father's maneuverings, "HBO had suddenly become the world's single largest financier of feature films."

Launching TV Land

JANE

My father could work magic with numbers—whether by hand or, eventually, with spreadsheets. This might have been overlooked by some top executives, but it drove profits. When Viacom launched TV Land, my father had a clever idea that outsmarted (almost) every cable operator and hauled in millions.

FRANK

When we launched TV Land in 1996, the executives at MTV Networks had a plan to add ten million subscribers in the first year. Normally we would charge the cable operators a monthly fee per subscriber ("per sub"), and in this case, we thought we could charge a nickel per sub.

So in the first year, this would net us around $3 million. Here's how the math works, and it requires a bit of nuance, as reality so often does: the plan was to *end* the first year with ten million subscribers, starting from a base of zero in January, and if you assume an even flow of growth, you'd use five million as the average base of subscribers for that first year. A monthly average of five million subs times 5 cents per sub times twelve months equals $3 million.

That's how it's normally done.

But instead we said, "Hey, why don't we try something different?"

Instead of charging cable operators 5 cents per TV Land sub, instead we went to them and said, "If you pay us the amount we're asking for Nickelodeon—40 cents per subscriber, per month—then you get TV Land for free!"

Now here's the fun part. We had been charging 35 cents per sub for Nickelodeon and were now asking for a 5-cent increase. Because Nickelodeon had a massive base of subscribers—sixty million—this translated to a far higher level of revenue for us than if we continued to charge 35 cents for Nickelodeon and added in 5 cents for TV Land subscribers. Under the proposed new scheme, yes, the cable operators got TV Land "for free," but if a base of sixty million subscribers paid the nickel increase . . . this would translate to $36 million in revenue for us—over ten times the original goal of $3 million.

So we went for it.

And what would you know, almost every cable operator happily paid it. The only one who declined was Brian Roberts, from Comcast, who laughed and said, "Do you think we didn't realize that you were suckering us into paying more than we might have normally paid, if you had done a conventional launch?"

I just laughed and said, "Hey, we had to try it." And it worked.

The Dilemma of Direct Broadcast Satellite (DBS)

In the long arc of the TV and media industry's history, the question that Dad and others tried to answer was this: What's the best way to deliver content to consumers? In the beginning, cable companies had something of a death grip on this power, as landlines were the only way into people's homes.

Then came satellite. At first, satellite technology was helpful to the cable companies, as it let them deliver their content to rural areas that couldn't be accessed by cable alone. (Satellite would carry the signal part of the way, and then cable the rest of the way.) But then satellites loomed as competition. Satellites, or Direct Broadcast Satellite (DBS), its official name, could be seen as either an opportunity or a threat. In this story, it's clear which path the cable companies took.

One of the great convictions at HBO in the early '80s was that our distribution was somewhat restricted by the cable industry's land coverage, which tended not to do a very good job in low-density population areas. Meaning if you lived in a rural area, you couldn't necessarily get cable if you wanted it. And even if you had access to cable, customers had to buy the basic cable package before they could also subscribe to HBO or Showtime.

So around that period of time, we at HBO were approached by a developer who claimed there was a Canadian satellite, Anik, that was not being used but was in orbit, and under the existing treaties between the countries, it could be re-tilted so it would broadcast its signal to the United States.

We did a little bit of homework, and we spent some time with our Washington, DC, Federal Communications Commission (FCC) counsel, and they got comfortable enough that yes, indeed, all of that could happen. And the developer really wanted to grow it into a national, direct-to-the-home satellite business that would broadcast the video signal into a dish that was just under thirty-six inches.

Along the way, we brought General Electric (GE) into the discussion; the point person from GE was a young ex-naval nuclear navy officer named Kevin Sharer, who later went on to become CEO of Amgen, where I served on the board for fifteen years. At the time, he was doing the analytic work for GE, and then, simultaneously, Prudential Insurance expressed some interest in coming into the venture.

Now the problem, structurally, was that we had a sister company within Time Inc. called Time Inc. Cable, which ultimately became

Time Warner Cable (now Spectrum). They were often at joint planning and strategy sessions, and they were exposed to our strategies as we were exposed to theirs.

But when they heard about this direct-to-the-home venture, they felt concerned and basically called some of their brethren in the cable business who were a bit bigger than they were, who, in turn, called the powers that be at Time Inc. and basically said, "If you go through with this direct-to-the-home, we'll do everything in our power to ruin your business and make life miserable."

Our corporate bosses were a bit more conservative than we were at HBO, and they figured that the bird in the hand—the cable industry—was better than two in the bush, which would have been cable plus a nascent direct-to-the-home business. And they forced us to drop out of the joint venture, which essentially killed it.

That was the first time that it happened, but it wasn't the only time, where the cable industry—understandably—was defending what it believed to be its marketplace, and its exclusivity in that marketplace.

And this certainly wasn't our only adventure with DBS, and sometimes these moves led to the brink of international diplomatic crises.

At one point we made an investment—along with some partners—to position a satellite that could broadcast to Europe, which could expand HBO's business outside of the US. Specifically, our partner had an agreement with the government of Luxembourg, which would bring the satellite in Luxembourg orbital space.

But as we got closer to the launch date, and very near the twelfth hour, I got a call from the prime minister of Luxembourg.

"I'm most apologetic," the prime minister said, and I'm paraphrasing, "but I'm going to have to ask you to sell back your equity stake in this DBS project. The French government has just informed us that if we launch this service with Home Box Office, then France will turn off Radio Television Luxembourg." He pointed out that Radio Television Luxembourg was a big contributor to the nation's budget.

I recognized that the prime minister was in a tough spot. So we agreed to his ask, and we sold back our equity interest in the satellite. And several years later, that went on to become the base satellite for Sky, with the enormously successful Western European DBS service, now part of Comcast.

JANE

Piggybacking on my father's thoughts, they continued to defend their turf long beyond satellite, and to internet distribution, too. But innovation will always find a way if it is better (or cheaper) for the customer. The newest irony? Cable's best competitive asset in the US is that they also control the infrastructure that delivers the broadband internet into many people's homes, and as long as that holds true, they'll hold a seat at the table.

But that might change. If a country or municipality decided to provide internet access as a regulated utility—or even as a public good—the cable company's model could be doomed. COVID-19 has shown the need for equal access to the internet for education, business, or just a Zoom call with family, so this will be a fascinating dynamic to watch over the coming years in the media business.

And if you think this has no relevance to the future? In January 2021, Bloomberg reported that Elon Musk and Jeff Bezos, the world's two richest men at the time, were "duking it out before U.S. regulators over celestial real estate for their satellite fleets," as both planned to use satellites to zap internet service around the globe. What started out years ago as concern about satellites over Luxembourg has morphed into fleets of satellites across the planet. Seeking ways to widely distribute content has become a more timeless theme than you might have thought.

Doing My Own Work

JANE

My father's stories tend to come from the CEO's office, but to show how easily this applies to jobs of all stripes, I'll share how I've incorporated this mindset in my own career. In a role that wasn't exactly financial, I once volunteered to track the invoices paid and money left to spend from multiple corporate budgets—not exactly the glamour gig. But that gave me an edge when it came time to negotiate a high-profile new deal that involved projecting future spending and savings against those budgets. I knew the details cold. And when I used that knowledge to fill a key need at a critical moment, it helped my company secure a highly coveted twenty-year partnership. This earned me credibility. And it unlocked future opportunities.

Another example: When I started a new role, I made a cheat sheet of our largest divisions to help me learn, noting some key metrics in a spreadsheet: What percentage of overall revenue did each division contribute? What percentage of profits? Profit per employee? If I were my boss, where would I prioritize my time and attention? And so on. No one asked me to do this, but it helped me understand the company's puzzle pieces and how they snapped together and how they had changed over time. My father taught me that by nailing the things you can control, you can separate from the pack.

This is the advice I often give to young professionals early in their career. Before you have unique skills or experience, the things you can control are: 1) your level of preparation; 2) your willingness to learn (both the big stuff and the small stuff); and 3) following through on your commitments. Many young professionals focus on what's next and what they want, as opposed to hunkering down and earning that next opportunity by doing the work right in front of them.

CHAPTER 4

Listen First

Many of Dad's successes materialized because he was willing to listen to what people were really trying to accomplish, their "why." He was an outstanding listener, and in business, listening can be an overlooked superpower.

This is a power he used when he had the chance to acquire Merv Griffin Enterprises. Merv Griffin was a powerhouse in television for decades. The guy was a larger-than-life personality. And even if the name Merv Griffin doesn't ring too many bells, you'll recognize some of the shows he created, including *Jeopardy!* and *Wheel of Fortune*.

I had the chance to meet Merv a few times over the years. He helped us surprise Dad at his fiftieth birthday party. One summer, when I was a teenager, Merv invited us on his over-the-top yacht, "The Griff." He gave me a sweatshirt from the yacht's crew uniform with an embroidered "The Griff" logo—a silver and blue griffin—that I still have to this day.

My father and Merv struck a lucrative business deal worth hundreds of millions of dollars, and a long-term friendship was born. Merv agreed to the deal because my father asked him directly—he was always direct and never played mind games—what he wanted, and truly *listened* to his needs. It's amazing how simple negotiating can be when you stop playing games. The only games my father liked to play were *actual* games (like tennis).

The Merv Griffin Deal

JANE

Dad liked to avoid the spotlight, but that wasn't always possible in the '80s. "The December 1984 edition of *Esquire* magazine was devoted to 'The Best of the New Generation—The Men and Women Under Forty Who Are Changing America.' Biondi was one of those included in *Esquire*'s list," writes George Mair in *Inside HBO*. "He is described as a tough negotiator and smart financier who guided HBO during some of its best money making years without putting his own interests ahead of HBO or his HBO colleagues." So he could be recognized in a crowd . . . by people like Merv.

FRANK

If you're old enough, you might remember the old HBO "movie intro" music from the '80s. It's that music that swells to a crescendo as the HBO logo, in what was then cutting-edge 3D, is dramatically showcased from every angle. "*Dun, dun, dun-dun-dun! Dun-dun-dun! Dun-dun dun! Dun-dun DUN!*"

I knew that music well. Back in the early '80s, when I was still the CEO of HBO, I had traveled to a resort in Scottsdale, Arizona, to play in a charity tennis tournament. I was eating breakfast with my wife. At the table next to us, someone was humming that familiar HBO theme—*dun-dun-dun!* We turned to see who was humming.

Merv Griffin.

He looked at me and smiled. "Did I get it right?"

We both laughed. We introduced ourselves, and this started a friendship that lasted until Merv passed away. We played tennis together, shared the occasional dinner, and grabbed lunch whenever I was in LA or he was in New York.

Merv was an easy guy to like. Just one small example: if we happened to be at a hotel bar, the other guests would swarm Merv and ask him to get behind the piano. Even when he was pushing seventy—and you'd think he'd be tired of all that—Merv loved to entertain and he would happily oblige.

In 1986, I was at Coca-Cola and we had acquired Embassy (a story I told in the previous chapter), but we still wanted to grow through more acquisitions.

I got a call from Merv's agent, Lou Weiss, who was then the vice chairman of William Morris. "Where are you?" Lou asked.

"I'm in Los Angeles at the moment."

"Do you have any lunch plans?"

"I don't."

"Merv would like to have lunch with you."

"Fine. Just name the time and the place."

I then expected Lou to provide some details about lunch. Instead he said, "Merv has decided to sell the company, and he'd like to talk to you about potentially buying it."

The Merv Griffin company, at the time, included of course *The Merv Griffin Show*, as well as two workhorse game shows that had been running on network television for years. One was *Wheel of Fortune*. The other was *Jeopardy! Wheel* had just launched into syndication, and *Jeopardy!* was about to hit syndication. And Merv wanted to sell?

Interesting . . .

I drove across LA to meet Merv for lunch. He wanted to meet at his office, at Sunset and Vine, and he wasn't alone. The room was packed with people who worked for Merv—lawyers, assistants, agents.

Merv was excited about these two new syndicated shows of his, and he conveyed his optimism. He told me that he was planning on winding down *The Merv Griffin Show*. And now he was ready to sell the company, to cash in his chips.

Then I did something that most negotiators don't do. I asked questions and listened.

"Merv, what do you want?" I asked him. "What do you think the company is worth?"

"I want $250 million."

I nodded, thought about it for a second, and did some rough math in my head. "Okay, give me an idea of what you earned."

"Last year, I earned $6 million after taxes," Merv said from behind his desk. "But this year, I think we'll do $60 million pretax."

Again, I did some quick math. For those not familiar with this stuff, it's easy for these types of numbers—$250 million, $60 million, $2 billion—to feel hopelessly abstract and almost meaningless. But the truth is that in some ways it's pretty simple. Without getting too deep in the weeds, if Merv's company brought in $60 million of profit, which would likely increase, this felt like a good deal.

You add up all of the discounted profit estimates—Year 1 + Year 2 + Year 3, and so on—and that's basically what the company should be worth. There's more nuance to it, but that's the general idea, and it's true whether you're talking hundreds of dollars or billions of dollars; the logic is the same. If you're good at estimating the value of something that costs $1,000, you're probably good at estimating the value of something that costs $1 billion.

Back to Merv. If his annual profit was $6 million, then there was no way that the company was worth anything close to $250 million. But if his profit was really *$60 million*? Then even on a back of the envelope, I could sense that $250 million was a bargain. The deal would pay for itself in five years, give or take, and then give us a stream of income for who knew how many years to come—everything else would be gravy.

I kind of smiled to myself and said, "Listen, Merv. If you can demonstrate to us that you're going to do $60 million pretax, we'll pay you $250 million."

"Hey, let's do it!" Merv said.

We shook hands and ate lunch, but we both knew the deal was contingent on due diligence, and I had to clear it with my boss, Fay Vincent, then the head of the Coca-Cola Entertainment Business Sector (and future commissioner of Major League Baseball).

We crunched the numbers, and the math checked out. We were in the short strokes of getting a deal done, but Vincent insisted on getting a $2 million discount.

That $2 million—which sounds like a lot of money, and sure, it *is* a lot of money—was really only 1 percent of the total deal. This 1 percent threatened to blow up the entire acquisition. Vincent wouldn't budge. Even though I viewed the deal as having enormous upside and something of a no-brainer, he insisted on that $2 million. And Merv, understandably, stuck to his guns on the $250 million; he felt (rightly) that he was offering a fair price.

Stalemate.

So I returned to our late-night negotiating session with Merv and his people. I said to Merv, "You have a company airplane, don't you?"

"Yeah."

"What's it worth?"

"Two million dollars."

"Okay. Why don't you keep the plane, and we'll pay you $2 million less. And anytime you want, you can charter it back to the company."

"Sure, sounds great."

We had a deal.

Why did it work out so smoothly? Part of it was just because Merv and I were friends, and in the entertainment business—or any business—your personal relationships can make or break a deal. Yet there was a more subtle principle at play here. One of the most underrated skills in business, from the boardroom to the mailroom, is the simple act of listening.

Most people are not good listeners. Just by nature I tend to be more reactive, a counter-puncher. (That's how I play tennis, too.) My prejudice is to gather the facts before I opine on things. If I had first said to Merv, "We're only going to pay you $X million" and gave him some lowball number, that would have led to a long and contentious negotiation. In my experience, you can learn a ton just by keeping your ears open, instead of telling everybody how the world looks to you. So at the start of most negotiations, I do more listening than talking.

There was one more wrinkle. Merv was wrong about his $60 million pretax income for that year. His estimate was off by quite a bit.

Merv's company didn't earn $60 million . . . it earned $115 million, as *Wheel of Fortune* and *Jeopardy!* became the juggernauts that continue to run today, some thirty-five years later. To Merv's credit he never looked back, and I never met a guy who more enjoyed the proceeds of selling his business. He remained a friend until his death, and Sony, which later bought the Coca-Cola entertainment properties, is still the proud owners of *Wheel of Fortune* and *Jeopardy!*

Decades later, in hindsight, this was probably one of the greatest acquisitions in the history of the industry.

Castle Rock and a Deal about Nothing

JANE

As this story illustrates, the reality of "blockbuster deals" is different from the Hollywood dramatizations, and the biggest of deals can hinge on the tiniest of details. My father had a steel-trap memory for things like theatrical distribution fees, and his confidence in those percentages, ultimately, is what brokered one of the most consequential deals in the entertainment industry's history. This behind-the-scenes work rarely makes headlines, but in the upper echelons of the media industry, there are those who know. This story, for me, captures the essence of my father's contributions to the entertainment industry, and how he influenced an entire generation of TV watchers . . . even if they don't know his name. At the time Dad was still at Coca-Cola, still hungry to expand, and still willing to listen.

FRANK

The phone rang. It was Alan Horn. "I've decided to leave Fox," he said.

This was in 1987, and Alan had been a friend for several years. Much later, he would serve as the chairman of Walt Disney Studios.

But back in the eighties, he was running the movie division of 20th Century Fox, and before that he ran the show at Embassy. When Coca-Cola had acquired Embassy during my tenure there, we hoped to retain Alan, but he had left for Fox.

"I'm going to go with Rob, Martin Shafer, Andrew Scheinman, and Glenn Padnick," he told me (all old Embassy hands). The "Rob" was the director Rob Reiner, who was red hot—he had just helmed *Stand By Me* and *The Princess Bride.* "And we're going to form a company called Castle Rock."

I kept listening.

"We're looking around for funding," said Alan. "And we're hoping that Coke might be an interested party."

"Sure," I said. "What'd you have in mind?"

"Well, I've got a couple of conditions," he said, and then described his plan: they wanted to do TV pilots every year, and a guarantee of fifteen films, three a year, for the first five years that they were in business. "So I need, #1, your agreement we can make features," he continued. "And #2, distribution terms for both TV shows and films."

I used my go-to strategy: ask questions and listen. "First off, how much money are we talking about?"

"Well, we only need about $30 million in equity, and that would get you about 40 percent of Castle Rock."

Here was my logic: I thought these were some of the best half-hour comedy guys working, so I was more than happy to make the investment in TV. Their track record included developing *Diff'rent Strokes, The Facts of Life,* and *Who's the Boss.* The movies were a bit trickier, but we knew that out of the fifteen films, we'd get at least four Rob Reiner films—maybe five, assuming he did one a year—so we were pretty confident we weren't going to get killed.

"Look, Alan, we'll put in the $30 million, happily, for 40 percent. We can do standard theatrical and TV distribution fees, assuming Castle Rock puts up its own production and marketing costs."

For a moment we need to dive into the details of distribution fees. Just like with discount rates at Embassy, this is the stuff that ultimately swings billion-dollar decisions. Let's say that Castle Rock makes a movie. We (at Coca-Cola Entertainment) would distribute it for them. Our cut was the distribution fee. The higher the fee, the better for us and the worse for Alan.

One bit of nuance: we also had a "favored nations" contract with certain clients, meaning that we were bound, contractually, to give them the lowest possible fee that we offered. So, if we offered Alan something better, we had no choice but to give it to our Favored Nation clients.

"That's a good offer," Alan told me on the phone. "We have one or two other people to talk to, but let me get back to you."

Two weeks went by.

He called me back to say that Universal Studios had offered the same standard theatrical distribution fee, but also a 2.5 percent lower *television* distribution fee. That was . . . kind of crazy.

"Gee, Alan, who are you working with?" I asked him.

"Tom Pollock."

Tom was a renowned Hollywood lawyer who later went on to run Universal Pictures, but he didn't run TV. Something didn't add up. I knew there was no way they would authorize a TV fee that low.

"Look, Alan, I don't know how they're doing that. They have the same issues that we do. Just be careful you're not getting bait and switched."

"Okay," said Alan. "But if you can't match it, we're going to have to go with him."

For maybe a fraction of a second I thought about getting angry. We had made a good offer, a fair offer, and we were the first ones to do so. I couldn't see how Universal could *possibly* be serious about their offer. But I kept my cool. "All right. Good luck." Despite the souring of the deal, I hung up the phone on good terms—there's rarely a reason to leave a negotiation on bad terms. The entertainment industry is small, and you'll work with the same people over and over.

Ten days later Alan called me back.

"You were right," he said. It turned out that the head of TV at Universal—who had not been consulted—appealed to the CEO, and Tom Pollock was overruled, and their too-good-to-be-true offer was changed, no surprise, to the standard fees we offered. "Since you guys were the first to make that offer . . . Are you still interested in doing Castle Rock?"

"You bet."

We had a deal, did the paperwork, and Castle Rock opened for business. Two years prior to this, my staff at Coca-Cola had been a secretary and assistant. By this time, thanks to the acquisitions of Merv Griffin, Embassy, and Castle Rock, it had swelled to include seven hundred employees and made $275 million in profit.

Castle Rock's first film, a comedy called *When Harry Met Sally*, was a solid success, but their second film, a remake of *Lord of the Flies*, was underwhelming. Maybe we had made the wrong bet?

Then came *Misery*, *City Slickers*, *A Few Good Men*, *In the Line of Fire*, *The Shawshank Redemption*, and a litany of other classics. Suddenly $30 million looked like the steal of the century.

The irony was, I had mostly made the deal for their TV business, but their early pilots did not take off as quickly. For example, just one of their eight pilots in 1989 ended up succeeding. A couple of years later, after I had moved from Coke to Viacom (that's another story entirely), I still stayed in touch with Martin Shafer and the other Castle Rock partners, just to see how they were doing, and he told me about that successful pilot from 1989.

One day over tennis, I asked Martin, "Hey Marty, how's your TV business doing?"

"You wouldn't believe it! We sold a show to NBC," he said.

Apparently some guy, some comedy writer, was living in his car—actually *living in his car*—when he sold the show to Castle Rock, and Castle Rock sold it to NBC.

"What's it about?" I asked Marty.

"It's about nothing."

Apparently, it was written by a comedian named Larry David, it starred his co-creator, a comedian named Jerry Seinfeld, and you know the rest.

"How Should We Spend $10 Million?" (by Tom Freston)

JANE

Tom Freston, who appears frequently in this book, was the head of all MTV Networks at one time, reporting directly to Dad at Viacom. His story illuminates how my father and the team focused on new content that they originated—a precursor to the Netflix era. And it's a listening story told from the perspective of the person who was listened to!

TOM

Early in Frank's reign at Viacom, we had an off-site in Woodstock, Vermont. There were maybe fifty or so people from senior leadership. We were under a lot of debt at the time and didn't have much extra cash or capital. So at the off-site, Frank said, "We're only going to have $10 million of extra capital to invest in *one thing*. We want all you guys to go away in your own groups and come back, and tell us, if you had $10 million, what would you do?"

We went away in our groups and then came back and said, "The single best thing we could do with $10 million is to beef up Nickelodeon." We had been licensing a lot of animation that we didn't really own. But if we could develop our own animation studio? And create our own characters? And what if we could do it in an untraditional way—not the Hanna-Barbera factory way—but instead find individual animators who had been approaching us, who had characters living inside of them, and give *them* a break? Then we would own the characters.

So at the Woodstock off-site, everyone presented their ideas, and we made the case that if we beefed up Nickelodeon we would be like a studio, creating something we owned, so we wouldn't have to worry about paying licensing fees. Most importantly, we could develop a licensing product and merchandising business, which is where a lot of the money was in children's television.

Our idea won out. So we created *Ren & Stimpy*, a show called *Doug*, and *Rugrats*. This set in place a business that would, over the years, generate billions of dollars. Nickelodeon really became the financial lynchpin of the MTV Networks. MTV might have gotten the headlines, but Nickelodeon was always number one in the ratings.

We created *SpongeBob*, and *Dora the Explorer*, and of course *Beavis and Butt-Head*—so many characters that generated billions and billions of dollars in licensing revenue.

And all of this started from contests that Frank put in place—very transparently—where everybody vied for the only $10 million that we had. Frank was an early believer in us, and he made it clear.

For the whole time that Frank was at Viacom, he ran the business with a light touch, but it was a smart touch. He got that we were not a traditional division. He understood there was a special sort of DNA at this place, and he knew that we didn't really want to be part of a big company to begin with. We wanted to operate sort of as our own little island within Viacom, and he let that happen.

And he gave us a lot of creative freedom. He would never opine on whether we should do this or that; he would really listen.

More Ado about Nothing

JANE

When my father shared the story about *Seinfeld*, he understated one important aspect of the deal: his own sense of fairness and how that contributed to the new partnership's goodwill. This story, like many, could have just as easily been categorized as Live with Integrity.

After the potential deal at Universal went bust, the truth, as Alan Horn later told me, is that my father had them over a barrel. "We had no leverage. It was over, and we were running out of money," Alan Horn remembers. "We were in trouble."

Since my father now had the leverage, he could have tightened the screws on the deal and insisted upon more favorable terms for Coca-Cola. "Frank had every opportunity to squeeze us a little more, but instead he said, 'I'll give you the exact same deal I offered you before you went away,'" says Alan. "And we just loved that. He could have tweaked here and tweaked there, and he didn't do it."

Another key player from the deal, Martin Shafer, has a similar recollection. "We said to Frank, who's the most straightforward guy in the world, 'Look, the Universal deal is a little bit better deal for us,'" says Martin. As he remembers it, my father said to him: "I'll tell you what's going to happen. You're going to get in a conversation with Universal, and you're going to go down the road and down the road and down the road, and then they're going to try to change the deal on you, because you have nowhere else to go."

And then how did it play out? "What happened was exactly what he had said," says Martin. "So we went back to Frank." Then Martin adds, amazingly, "I can't remember exactly what it was, but I think he made our deal a little bit better. And we had no other place to go." Martin was right, what Dad ultimately offered the Castle Rock team turned out to be more equity for a smaller stake in the company than their competing offer.

After my father died, Rob Reiner wrote my mom a note that said, "I'll be forever grateful to him for his wisdom and guidance in helping us realize Castle Rock. It allowed me to do the best work of my life."

My father also understated the financial significance of the deal, and of *Seinfeld*. "It's the most successful show in the history of television. I don't think there's any question about it," says Alan Horn. It's hard to quantify exactly, but Martin Shafer's understanding is that the Sony ownership of Castle Rock—and Sony purchased the Coca-Cola entertainment business that my father built—has generated close to $1 billion.

In other words, my father's investment of $30 million into Castle Rock has yielded $1 billion since . . . from *Seinfeld* and all of the classic films they made such as *The Shawshank Redemption*, *The Green Mile*, *City Slickers*, and *When Harry Met Sally*. All because my father listened to Alan Horn and invested in a team that he believed in.

CHAPTER 5

Partner for the Long Term

JANE

In any negotiation, it's human nature to want the very best deal you possibly can, squeezing every last drop from your counterpart. If you can run up the scoreboard? Even better. Plenty of brash negotiators live by the adage of CRUSH YOUR OPPONENT.

My father took a different path. He had a saying: "Make sure both sides get some wins." That way, you leave the door open for doing more business in the future.

"Frank was really cool all the time. He was always calm and reasoning," says Alan Schwartz, the former CEO of Bear Stearns who knows a little something about negotiating. Alan explains that my father's cool demeanor—and willingness to give the other side some wins—actually made him a more effective negotiator, because after he accrued some goodwill, he would see more deals in the future, such as Jerry Perenchio and Embassy.

Alan contrasts my father's approach with the negotiating style of other, more hard-headed CEOs (including a famous one I'll respectfully leave anonymous) who always try to squeeze the other side. Yes, the *crush your opponent* approach might fetch you a bit of extra value in the short term, but it has a long-term cost: You miss out on deals because no one wants to work with you again. "On the other hand," says Alan, "Frank Biondi saw every deal."

My father's negotiating style—fair, genial, decent—was just one of the many ways he built long-term relationships. Dad partnered for the long term—in all areas of his life. He was married to my mom for more than forty-five years on the day he died. He maintained lifelong friendships. And when it came to his professional life, he understood that relationships are often the keys to success. "People like to work with people who they like and trust," he used to say. I can hear him saying this as I write.

Think about a business deal. If you view it as just a "transaction," then you are not concerned with what happens at the end of the deal or what happens to your counterparty. It's purely functional. But if you view it as a relationship and partnership, then there's more long-term value to be created. In a world that is increasingly becoming more moment-to-moment transactional, there's merit to thinking about the longer term.

These long-term partnerships could lead to surprising break-throughs. If my father had trust in a solid team, then he could take a leap of faith that the things they would create—which might, at the time, be hard to visualize—would eventually deliver results. Any successful venture capitalist does the same thing. Some whiz-bang invention could be the "next big thing," but if the founders are a bunch of clowns? Pass. To build off a story from the previous chapter, in 1987, my father couldn't exactly envision *Seinfeld* . . . but he believed in and invested in the people who could.

Expect the Unexpected

Jon Dolgen, the former chairman of Viacom Entertainment Group featured in this story, would become one of my father's best friends. As I wrote about in the prologue, just before my dad passed away, Jon and his wife Susan visited him to pay final respects and listened to the recording of Dad telling this story. "I love this man," he recently said. "I love him." But their relationship got off to a rocky start, and this is a story Dad loved to tell.

FRANK

In 1982, when I was at Home Box Office, we discovered that Columbia, 20th Century Fox, and CBS were entering into a deal to buy Showtime. The powers that be at our parent company, Time Inc., all agreed that we should do everything necessary to prevent that from happening, so that HBO could maintain its dominant market share.

So we contacted Columbia Pictures, who agreed that they would enter into a forty-eight-hour negotiation that, if successful, would preempt their participation in the purchase of Showtime, and probably kill the deal.

We started on a Sunday. We'd go through Monday, and then the deadline, to my recollection, was early on Tuesday morning, when they were going to sign the Showtime deal.

Now Columbia, at that point in time, had what was considered to be the fiercest negotiator in all of Hollywood, in the person of Jonathan Dolgen. It was in Jon's blood; his dad was a labor negotiator. When Jon walked into a negotiating room, his custom was to break out five packs of cigarettes, several packs of Juicy Fruit gum, assorted candies, and Rolaids.

Jon was ably assisted by Chase Carey, who went on to run a number of enterprises including DIRECTV and Formula One, and Tom McGrath, who ultimately became chief administrative officer of Paramount Pictures, but it was Jon's custom to handle all the negotiations. It was our custom to rotate three of us: Steve Scheffer, our film acquisition executive; Michael Fuchs, our programming executive (and later the head of HBO); and myself . . . with Jon, in what amounted to straight twenty-four-hour-through negotiations.

The first day was disappointing. We accomplished virtually nothing, and it didn't seem like we were making any progress toward realizing a huge film output deal for Columbia, and the creation of TriStar Pictures.

On Monday morning, we got a call from Jerry Levin, our boss in the video group at Time Inc., saying he knew we were locked in this make-or-break negotiation, but he had to see us—all three of us, the negotiators—at two p.m. that day, and that we should pick a proxy negotiator who could sit in for us for half an hour.

So we looked around, and our deputy general counsel was a young woman named Leslie Jacobson who handled all the film acquisition legal work. We said to Leslie, "We're going to put you in the chair at ten this morning, and just try and hold your own. I mean, this is not an enviable position for anybody to go into against Jon, who is just a fierce negotiator."

"Okay, I'll do my best," Leslie said. Leslie went in the chair at ten, and we hung around to see how she did.

We'd feared that Leslie might falter, but, amazingly, within fifteen minutes, she had won three points that we had been unable to win in the last twenty-four hours. As time went on, more and more points were getting decided, and it became apparent that if this continued, it was entirely possible that we might actually get a deal structured.

In the end, we were able to conclude the negotiations. TriStar Pictures was formed, a huge output deal was put together with Columbia Pictures, and Showtime was never purchased by the studios and CBS.

Jon's boss, Victor Kaufman (the general counsel at Columbia pictures), was so impressed at the job Leslie had done that he came to us and said, "TriStar is going to need a general counsel. Would you have any objection if I offered the job to Leslie?"

"Hey, be our guest," we said. "She's a big girl. She can say yes or no." And she ultimately went over there and spent several years as general counsel, before returning to HBO.

And as for Jon Dolgen? Because we worked with mutual respect, he and I were able to develop a long-term relationship. Ultimately, he came to work for us at Viacom, running Paramount and doing a fabulous job. We've been close friends for decades.

A Message from the King

JANE

My father never name-dropped, bragged about the people he knew, or talked about celebrities. Which is why, during a family vacation, it was so surprising to hear Don King talk about my dad before a marquee pay-per-view fight. Dad took these family trips *seriously*—as important as any business deal, as he marked family vacations on a calendar and fiercely guarded the dates. His most important long-term "partnership" was always family.

FRANK

When I was at HBO in the early 1980s, I worked with Don King. This was before pay-per-view fights really took off, and we had a long-term boxing relationship. I enjoyed working with Don.

By the end of that decade, I was at Viacom—which then owned Showtime—and I read that HBO had formed a venture with Don King to do pay-per-view fights. At Showtime we had very much the same idea, but not necessarily with Don as the promoter.

Later we got word that Don and HBO were at odds over the pay-per-view terms. Don called us. He said that he was finished at HBO, and he wanted to know if we (at Showtime) would be interested in talking to him about a long-term relationship. I said sure.

So we set up a pay-per-view deal with Showtime, somewhat over the amazement of our general counsel, Philippe Dauman (who would years later become the CEO). "Wait a minute," Philippe said, "this man's a felon."

I laughed and said to Philippe, "We've done business with Don for a long time. And we've also done business with Bob Arum, who's a Harvard Law School graduate, and also a top-notch fight promoter."

I told Philippe that on a day-to-day basis, it was much easier to do business with Don than it was with the Harvard guy. Don paid slowly, but he always paid, and he was one of those rare individuals who you could shake hands with and you had a deal. Sometimes it was a little too cute by half, but you still had a deal.

Now on a personal front, one thing I've always done through the course of my career—at HBO, Coca-Cola, then Viacom—was go skiing as a family, most often in Vail. I've always said that one of the most important parts of leadership is taking the time to recharge, to find balance, and for me that meant spending time with family. And at Viacom, we sponsored a large sales meeting every winter, held in Vail, that we called CarniVail. As part of this sales meeting, we would hire 100 to 150 ski instructors to work with the guests. We got to know and like these ski instructors. But we never talked about work or Viacom; one of the beauties of these vacations was that even when you skied with the instructors, they really had no idea what you did on a day-to-day basis.

In the late 1990s, after I parted ways with Viacom, I happened to be skiing in Vail with my family. At the time there was a huge pay-per-view fight with Mike Tyson on a Saturday night. (I didn't see it.) But on Sunday, we met our ski instructors on the base lift, as usual. For some reason they were all atwitter.

"What's going on?" I asked.

"You know Don King?" the ski instructors asked, in a bit of awe.

"Yes, I know Don King. Why?"

"Did you see the fight last night?"

"No."

Apparently Don King had publicly thanked me for the Showtime relationship and sung my praises.

I just smiled and said, "Well, that's just Don in a nutshell."

JANE And that was just *Dad* in a nutshell . . . matter-of-fact, unassuming, quick to downplay any praise.

No Profit in Holding Grudges

JANE

Dad never forgot what happened to him at the start of his career, when he interviewed for a job at Goldman Sachs, and how that experience played a factor in decisions he made twenty years later.

FRANK

After my second year of Harvard Business School, I decided to focus on investment banking. I'd like to say that this was a lifelong passion, but the truth is that no child dreams of becoming an investment banker. The real motivation: I was good at math, I liked finance, and no single industry struck me as the one that I wanted to work in. (The "entertainment industry" intrigued me, but at the time, it somehow didn't feel like a responsible way to make a living.) With investment banking, I didn't have to choose just one industry—I'd get exposure to a variety of companies and sectors.

So naturally I wanted to interview at Goldman Sachs, the undisputed industry leader. I didn't expect to land a job, as my grades were okay but not the top of the class. But I thought that maybe, after a good first interview on campus, they'd give me a shot at a follow-up interview in New York. I was also curious; what was the vaunted Goldman Sachs really like?

Harvard staged the interviews at the main teaching building, Aldrich Hall, in the alcoves of little hallways outside the classrooms. Curtains sealed off the tiny interview spaces. I arrived a few minutes early, waited for the candidate before me to leave, and then a Goldman partner popped his head around the curtain. We shook hands, he introduced himself, and then he sat back down.

"Look," he said right away, "I'm sorry to tell you that you can talk about anything you want, but we can't talk about Goldman Sachs."

Wait.

What?

"I can talk to you about anything—the Red Sox, the Yankees, sports, the weather—but not Goldman Sachs." He told me that

Goldman had a policy of only hiring Baker Scholars (the equivalent of Phi Beta Kappa), and I was not a Baker Scholar.

"You're kidding me, right?"

"That's just the way it is," he said. "We can sit here and chat, or if you'd like, you can take off."

Well, that was an easy choice. I did a 180 and left.

That was in 1968. Now wind the clock forward to 1988, when I was the CEO of Viacom.

Our CFO, Tom Dooley, marched into my office, a big smile on his face. "I just got a proposal from Goldman! They want to do a billion-dollar bond offering for us."

Some context: we had been doing a round of refinancing to get better terms so we'd pay less in interest on our debt every year, and a billion-dollar offering was a big deal, especially from Goldman. A firm like Goldman is picky. They only underwrite bonds for companies they believe to be rock solid. And to be candid, back then, Viacom wasn't exactly AAA material. We were viewed as an overleveraged, debt-strapped, second-rung media company. But that perception had begun to change. As we grew the MTV Networks, the industry started to take us more seriously. This is why Tom (our CFO) was so excited. If Goldman wanted to underwrite us? That would both A) secure us better financing terms (essentially, a lower interest rate), and B) serve as a real validation for the team's work. It would be a real feather in the cap.

Tom looked at me. "This is a big deal!"

"Tom, that's great. But let me tell you a story."

And I told him about my humiliating interview—*Sorry, kid, I can talk to you about the Yankees or the Red Sox, but not Goldman.*

The blood drained from his face. He later called his contact at Goldman, asked around, and he learned that the partner who had interviewed me—*Sorry, kid*—was notorious for this practice. By then, I had also learned that he had violated the rules for interviewing at Harvard Business School.

The next morning, I received a call from the co-COO of Goldman

Sachs, Steve Friedman, who would later serve as chairman of the New York Federal Reserve Bank.

"I don't know if I'm going to laugh or cry," Steve began. "We'd really like to do the business. I hope you can get past this. I'll do whatever you ask, within reason. If you want, I'll come up and kiss your ass in Times Square."

I thought for a second, trying not to laugh. "Let me talk it over with my colleagues, and we'll get back to you."

We waited a day to get back to Goldman, but the truth is that it wasn't a hard decision. It was simple. What they had done twenty years ago was a bit of a personal insult, but I had a larger duty to the Viacom shareholders—to see that they got the best financing possible. There's no profit in holding grudges. There was no need for a Times Square ass-kissing.

The reality of 1988 was that I knew Goldman would do an excellent job. Added bonus? This put a burr in their saddle to prove that while they had made a mistake, they were eager to make things right. I felt that they would knock the refinancing out of the park.

And they did. Goldman restructured the billion-dollar bond deal, gave us greater credibility, and helped to lower the interest rates between 4 and 5 points on a base of three billion dollars, saving us $150 million of interest expense each year.

So the next time you're made to feel small because you're not a "Baker Scholar"—or if you don't belong to a certain school or neighborhood or country club—know that there are more important ways to prove your worth.

What Goes Around, Comes Around: *Blade Runner* Negotiations

JANE

This story is about the long-term impact of acting with integrity (the theme from chapter 2). Integrity is not just about dramatic moments of right and wrong, but also overlooked acts of decency. In the negotiations for *Blade Runner*, my father's unwillingness to take a punitive, demolish-the-opponent position helped engender goodwill and set up a future deal that would be worth millions. Not only is doing the right thing the right thing, but it also translates to better results in the long run.

Sometime in the early '80s, HBO had licensed the film *Blade Runner*, which, even though it was not a box office success, had become a cult classic. We licensed directly from Embassy films, which was owned by Norman Lear and Jerry Perenchio. (This was before I acquired Embassy while at Coca-Cola.) Jerry had been dealing with our film acquisition group, which wound up paying, to my recollection, a license fee of half a million dollars.

About six months later, before we had actually run the movie on-air, it became apparent to Jerry that HBO had gotten a very good license deal. He called the head of Time Inc., Dick Munro, to complain.

"I don't do that," Dick said to him. "I'll transfer you down to Frank."

When we spoke, Jerry explained that he felt it just wasn't right. He felt that the film was a higher quality than the deal suggested, and that films of that quality had received higher license fees from HBO in the past.

I said, "All I can do, Jerry, is go talk to the licensing people and see if there's anything we can do."

After a series of conversations, we concluded that we could increase the license fee by $250,000, and hopefully everybody would feel better. So we did it. And Jerry was very appreciative. I didn't think much more of it, and I didn't know Jerry well, but he said, "Thank you and God bless."

This appreciation paid off several times over the years.

As luck would have it, after I left HBO, almost two years later, one of the first phone calls I received was from Jerry. He said, "I'd love to talk to you about selling our company, Embassy." He said that he hated investment bankers but had enjoyed doing business with me in the past.

That started a conversation. And when I started at Coca-Cola—heading up the entertainment acquisition business—Jerry was the first phone call I made, and we wound up buying Embassy, thanks to the magic of discount rates.

During my career, I came to realize the truth of "what goes around comes around." Yes, that can have a negative connotation, but happily, when you accumulate goodwill to build a partnership, what goes around comes around in the most serendipitous of ways.

CHAPTER 6

Hire Smart, Then Empower

JANE

Because Dad was working in what is often called a cutthroat industry, he frequently had the opportunity to think about what was the best way to lead. Do you need to be a ruthless CEO who—niceties be damned—wrings the best out of his or her team? Or a hands-on technocrat who personally inspects every detail? Or an inspiring visionary who seems to have a clairvoyant view of the future?

None of that is necessary. "Almost everything would fall under the general banner of common sense," my father once said when asked to describe his leadership style. "I don't think it's all that complicated, to be honest with you." He loved to speak plainly.

When it came to building a team and bringing out the best in others, Dad could be a master puppeteer. By analogy, some musicians like to surround themselves with dancers who aren't quite as good as they are so that they'll look like the star. My father took the opposite approach. He wasn't afraid of being outshone, and he had the confidence to recruit the absolute best. This was a rare approach in the entertainment industry.

That's the kind of freedom and trust that my father gave his staff. He created strong teams at HBO, at Viacom, and then at Universal.

"He had assembled a phenomenal team," remembers Ken Solomon, who my father had hired to run Universal Studios Television, and later The Tennis Channel. Ken says that because of all the star-studded talent that my father put in place, "We called it Camelot."

A look at my father's approach to management—particularly running Viacom—gives insight into how to create a culture for a winning team. My father wouldn't have called himself a "creative," yet his team was recognized and awarded for its creative spark, particularly its original programming content, which I discussed in chapter 1. Even though he was successful often, Dad would want a balanced picture presented, so this chapter talks about both successes and failures when it came to empowerment.

Unlocking Value at MTV

JANE

A core driver of growth at Viacom was my father's belief in the power of setting the right goals. "You have to make sure that you, as the CEO—and your division heads—are setting reasonable, reachable stretch goals each year," he once said. "The best way to debilitate a great organization is to set goals that are not achievable, just for the sake of challenging people." In this story he set the right goal and then trusted and empowered his team to conquer it.

FRANK

One of the principal attractions of the Viacom job was the MTV family of networks. In 1987, the basic cable networks—which had been considered an afterthought by the industry—were beginning to gain a lot of traction, as the cable industry built out to eighty million subscribers, and DIRECTV was coming into being. The potential for both subscriber fees and increased advertising was certainly apparent to me, if not beginning to become apparent to the industry as a whole.

So when I got to Viacom, one of the first things I did was change the reporting order for the MTV Networks. There had been two co-heads, Tom Freston and a second executive, and I concluded that we were better off with Tom as the head of all the MTV Networks, and his counterpart resigned when he didn't get the job. That turned out to be one of the best executive decisions I made while I was at Viacom—or maybe during my entire career.

During the first budgeting season, Tom had been telling me and Redstone how great the MTV Networks staff was, and how good they were in execution. They presented a budget that was aggressive—it called for an increase in revenues of about 15 percent—but the industry as a whole projected to average 17 percent growth. We questioned Tom as to why, with such an "excellent staff," the performance was going to be slightly below average to the industry.

To his credit, Tom hadn't realized that, and he said, "Let me get back to you." He proceeded to do a survey of both the cable industry and the advertising industry, on the effectiveness of the MTV Networks' staff. The results were somewhat surprising. The staff was rated somewhat in the middle—average to slightly below average.

Tom quickly took some action and replaced the head of affiliate relations (which dealt with the cable industry) and the head of ad sales, and he installed new executives across the line. He revised the budget to a more aggressive 20-odd percent growth. He started a process of unlocking serious revenue growth and earning potential for the MTV Networks, Nickelodeon, VH1, and ultimately all the other networks that we started, from Comedy Central to TV Land. And it became the growth engine of Viacom.

Pig in the City

JANE

While hiring then empowering led to excellent results in most cases, there were times when my father had to admit that he gave a creative team a little too much freedom and not enough oversight. Which brings us to this next story, from my father's time at Universal Studios.

How many times have you walked out of the movie theater and said, shaking your head, "What a disaster! Why the hell did they make that?"

Here's a story that will help explain.

No one sets out to make bad movies. Then again, no one has any illusion that all of them are winners. The typical head of a studio manages a portfolio of fifteen films. You might think that the job is to sift through all of the worthy projects, and then whittle a list of a thousand down to a hundred and then to twenty-five and then to curate the best fifteen. Except that's not how it works. For most execs in the film business, the thought is not, *Which fifteen should we pick?* but rather, *Boy, I hope I can find fifteen!*

There are usually only five or six quality projects a year that a studio feels good about.

You might ask the reasonable question, "Okay, if there are only five quality movies, why even bother with the other ten? Why not just make the five?"

Because the other ten movies *must* get made to cover the studio's overhead. Fundamentally, this is why so many mediocre movies get produced. A studio can't be profitable with only five titles. They need volume, but there are not enough high-quality concepts, so they trot out more films that just maybe, hopefully, will turn out better than expected. Every year it's a crapshoot.

This is why franchises are so coveted. With an *Avengers* or a *Star Wars* or a *Toy Story* (all, incidentally, now owned by Disney), you are guaranteed to fill the seats. It's a real luxury. For a studio exec staring at that roster of fifteen question marks, if three or four of them are surefire winners, suddenly the year is looking up.

This brings us to *Babe*.

When I arrived at Universal in 1996, we had one of the greatest gifts a studio could ever receive—an accidental franchise. *Babe* was a low-budget ($30 million) film about a talking pig that had grossed $254 million, was nominated for seven Academy Awards (including Best

Picture), and had millions of Americans quoting the line, "That'll do, pig. That'll do." *Babe* was directed by a relatively unknown Australian, Chris Noonan, who had shattered every expectation.

A sequel was a no-brainer. Universal had stumbled into a lucrative franchise that we could repeat with *Babe 2*, *Babe 3*, *Babe 4*, and into eternity. And that was just on the movie side. Think of the ancillaries! We could roll out Babe roller coasters at Universal Theme Park, Babe stuffed animals, Babe lunch boxes.

The movie itself, *Pig in the City*, seemed like the right kind of recipe for a sequel. To save the farm, our beloved pig needs to win a contest, and for that he must travel to the faraway city of Metropolis. It's a classic fish-out-of-water story, and it would take what people loved about the original and sprinkle in something new. This time we'd have a larger budget—$92 million vs. $30 million on the original.

As a bonus, *Babe 2* would be helmed by acclaimed director George Miller, of *Mad Max* fame. If the unknown Chris Noonan could belt a home run with a $30 million budget, just imagine what George Miller—a legend—could do with triple the resources. Miller shot the film in Australia. That didn't concern anyone, as Miller was from Australia, and that's where the original *Babe* had been shot too.

So what's it like to visit a movie set in Australia?

No idea. I never once visited the set. In fairness, that's not unusual; it's rare for the CEO to personally inspect the production. And I hadn't seen any footage.

This is why I didn't know what to expect when I sank into my chair at Universal's LA screening room, along with the other executives, and we saw it for the first time. Before the movie began, we all had some questions: Would we give it a marketing push for the Oscars? How much should we spend on *Babe 3*? Would George Miller want to direct again, or would we need to find someone new?

The lights in the screening room darkened. And then we sat in darkness, in every sense of the word, as the film depicted a dark, bleak, gritty, frightening city that would depress even the happiest child. It was scary. It was grim. It was, to be fair, perhaps exactly what you'd expect from the director of *Mad Max*.

As the end credits rolled I wondered, *Holy mackerel, is this thing as bad as I think it is? Are other people reacting the same way? Are we screwed?*

Yes, yes, and yes.

I looked at the other studio execs. We all asked the same question: what the hell had happened?

I learned that *none* of the studio execs had paid a visit to Australia. Not the head of our film studio. Not the senior producers. George Miller had been on his own. There was no studio feedback.

"How can we fix this?" I asked.

We couldn't.

It was too late to reposition, reshoot, or recut the movie. This bummer of a kids' movie would ship to the theaters as-is. Critics said that it was "laden with more useless pork than a congressional bill" and "a desperate, pathetic mess." As one critic said, "Despite its G-rating, the movie includes numerous scenes of animals in peril, including a pit bull that nearly hangs himself, a crippled dog that gets thrown into a wall and a goldfish that almost suffocates . . . Happy holidays, kids!"

Pig in the City opened on the long Thanksgiving weekend of 1998. Thanksgiving is traditionally a good weekend for family-friendly movies, and this year was no exception. On that five-day weekend of 1998:

A Bug's Life (Disney) earned $45.8 million.

The Rugrats Movie (Paramount) earned $27.4 million.

. . . And the dark, dystopian *Pig in the City* earned $8.2 million.

It would only make a total of $18 million domestic and $50 million foreign, a far cry from our supersized budget of $90 million. But the real cost was the lost opportunity of building a franchise. *Babe* should have been a reliable cash cow for years and even decades.

We snatched defeat from the jaws of victory. If *Babe 2* were an NFL game, it would be the 1978 match-up between the Eagles and

Giants. The Giants were up 17–12 with only a few ticks left on the clock. The Eagles were out of time-outs. Instead of just taking a knee, the Giants bizarrely handed off to the fullback . . . who fumbled. The Eagles picked up the ball and returned it for a touchdown. Eagles win. Every Giants fan screamed at the TV and wondered, *How'd that happen?* That was our reaction at Universal. *How could they have possibly screwed that up?*

The words "studio notes" often have a negative connotation, as we tend to hear from the creatives—the screenwriters and directors—who grumble about their vision being compromised. We rarely hear about the flip side, when the studio can keep a movie on track.

Eventually the head of our film division, Casey Silver, would be let go. (There were other misfires, such as *Meet Joe Black*.) But ultimately, this is the CEO's responsibility, and this is a lesson for any business leader. I made the mistake of giving my direct reports too much rope. Just a few years earlier, at Viacom, I had built a trusted team; we had open lines of communication, clear feedback loops, and they had earned their autonomy. I could delegate with confidence.

When I started at Universal, we lacked those trusted teams and lines of communication. It's one thing to empower your people and stay relatively hands off, but the pendulum can't swing too far the other way.

We worked to ensure that this could never happen again, that our execs were more hands-on, and that we would avoid *Babe 3: When the Pig Meets Hitler*, directed by Quentin Tarantino.

Learn When to Let Go

JANE

As the previous story showed, empowering others doesn't always lead to the best outcomes, which is a fact of life. But there were times when an employee's behavior was so out of line with the company that they had to be fired. As Sherry Lansing once said, "Frank might have had to let someone go, but he did it with such dignity, and such kindness, that people still liked him." Well . . . maybe they didn't *always* like him. Which brings us to my father's next story.

Dick Snyder was a legend in the publishing industry. For some historical perspective, when he began working at Simon & Schuster, the president of the United States was Dwight D. Eisenhower. In 1978, Snyder became CEO, and under his watch, Simon & Schuster's revenue grew from $30 million to $2 billion. He inked deals with a glittering list of Simon & Schuster authors such as Bob Woodward, Joan Didion, and Philip Roth. He grew it into the world's mightiest book publisher.

It's too bad I had to fire him.

In 1994, when our paths crossed, it's true that Snyder was a towering force. He was awed, respected, feared. He was the emperor. Yet it's also true and widely known that he, well . . . he acted a bit like an emperor. In the Simon & Schuster headquarters at Rockefeller Center, for example, each morning he commandeered his own private elevator—an assistant would shut down a public elevator when he approached the building and hold it until he arrived. He traveled by chauffeured limo. As *The New York Times* later put it, Snyder was the "Little Napoleon of publishing," who was both "despised and honored."[8]

And he hated Viacom, his new parent company. In Viacom's recent epic bidding war with QVC over Paramount, Dick was pulling for Barry Diller. He made no secret that he wanted nothing to do with Paramount, and nothing to do with Viacom.

Yet we had won. Diller lost. Viacom swallowed up Paramount, which meant that I was CEO of the combined company, and suddenly I was Dick Snyder's boss.

Shortly after the acquisition went through, my phone rang. Dick Snyder.

"Look, would you be willing to have lunch?" Dick told me that

---

8   Roger Rosenblatt, "See Dick Run, Again," *New York Times Magazine*, October 1, 1995.

he wanted to give his side of the story, and explain why he was so anti-Paramount.

"Sure."

"How about the Four Seasons?" Dick asked, perhaps not surprisingly, as the Four Seasons was then a famed location for midtown power lunches.

"Done."

We picked a date and made it happen. It was my habit to walk from Viacom's headquarters, on 7th Avenue, to the restaurants on Park Avenue for lunch. It's a nice walk. So on a clear, crisp, sunny spring day, I walked to the Four Seasons and met Dick for lunch.

We made small talk and then he got into it. The gist: Dick claimed that he preferred the other guys, Barry Diller and QVC, because he hated Marty Davis, the head of Paramount. And if Viacom won the bidding war, then Marty Davis would still be at the helm. (If Barry Diller had won, Davis would have been out.) I took all of this in. As always, it's my tendency to listen, observe, assimilate, and only then react.

"Davis mistreated me, personally," he said.

"To what end?"

"We were discriminated against." Dick explained that for the last three years, he believed Simon & Schuster had been treated differently than the other divisions of Paramount. "And they refused to negotiate an extension to my contract."

I took a bite of my entrée, giving it some quick thought. "Look, Dick, you know, this is all news to me. But just as a matter of curiosity, how old are you now?"

"Sixty-one."

"So if I can ask, what kind of extension to your agreement are you looking for?"

He told me he was expecting a six-year extension to his contract that had another four years to go. It was almost awkwardly long, given his age.

"Okay," I said. "This is all new information to me. Let me check with my people, and if there's validity to what you're saying, I'll happily make it right."

We finished our lunch cordially, picked up our coats, and walked out of the 52nd Street exit. We left the restaurant together, and then I spotted a Mercedes 600 sedan with a tall, white-gloved African American chauffeur. *Who's that for?* I thought. The chauffeur smoothly opened the door for Dick, who began to climb into the car.

I turned to walk back to the office. A moment of awkwardness. "Oh," said Dick, "can I give you a ride?"

Simon & Schuster—Dick's office—was just three blocks away. My office was five blocks away.

"Ah, sure," I said to be polite. "But just drop me off at Simon & Schuster, and I'll walk the rest of the way to Viacom."

You can learn a lot about someone by how they get to work.

When I returned to my office after the grueling two-block walk, I conveyed Dick's complaints to our financial and HR people. Twenty-four hours later I had my answers: There was absolutely no discrimination against Dick Snyder or the publishing company. Most of what he said at lunch, I realized, was just his wishful thinking.

That day I happened to hold a senior staff meeting, and I shared Dick's requests with the team. Then I learned some new information. Viacom's CFO and controllers had been calling their counterparts at Simon & Schuster to get updates on their performance—that's a given at a big corporation—and they would get stonewalled.

Dick wouldn't share the numbers. And he wouldn't let his people share the numbers. He would call the Viacom controllers back and say, in effect, *Why are you bothering my people? Leave me alone!*

I kept hearing more stories like this. Dick was feared and respected, yes, but he was also impossible to work with. The number one thing, the most important thing, at the highest levels of management is to surround yourself with good people, with people you trust. This is crucial when you're at the helm of a 150,000-employee conglomerate. And it was especially critical in this moment after the Paramount acquisition, when we needed people who were going to be on the team, philosophically.

Besides, life is too short to be fighting over something so basic as reporting your performance to corporate. You would be hard-pressed to find any public company that would tolerate that kind of behavior from an executive. The stakes are admittedly a bit lower, but it's similar to how, in 1951, President Truman wrestled with how to handle General Douglas MacArthur, who was extremely popular but aggressively insubordinate.

Back to the staff meeting. As the VPs and senior execs shared their frustrations with Dick's antics, there was one executive, in particular, who voiced his exasperation: Sumner Redstone.

"I just got a dinner invitation from that guy," said Sumner. "You know, I'm not particularly fond of him."

Others chimed in to agree.

"Well, why don't we just replace him?" Sumner asked.

I turned to Sumner. "Look, you've got my vote." After all, in the end, Truman was forced to fire MacArthur, no matter how bad it looked. I asked Sumner, "Would you like to do it?"

"No, no, no," he said, quickly backpedaling. "Why don't you and Philippe [Dauman, our general counsel] handle it?" I could sense right away that Sumner feared the blowback from the press. Dick Snyder was a popular figure in the media industry—he still is—and Sumner didn't want to be seen as the Bad Guy who axed a hero of publishing.

So instead it would fall to me along with Philippe to deliver the bad news. That's part of a CEO's job. I've been let go myself several times, so I know how it feels. Having been on the flip side, I try and do everything I can to lessen the sting of departure and to treat the person with dignity. We wanted to let Dick get the benefit of his current contract. We wanted to let him keep his stock options (granted several years prior), which could be worth a substantial amount of money. We wanted to let him leave with grace.

Philippe and I asked Dick to come over for a meeting, ostensibly to discuss the budget. His chauffeur drove him the few blocks to our offices at Viacom. He took a seat.

"Look, we're just going to have to let you go," I told him, as it's best to be straightforward and direct. "You don't seem comfortable doing business the way we're comfortable doing business."

Dick . . . did not take it well.

He erupted like a volcano.

"You sons of bitches!" He sprang from his seat and unleashed a torrent of profanity. I forget each and every word, but it amounted to, *Fuck you! Fuck all of you! Go fuck yourselves!*

I tried to keep my cool, and I wanted him to know that we would let him publicly save face. He could leave on friendly terms, and with minimal financial pinch. "We'll give you a consulting agreement for as long as a year," I told him.

"Fuck you."

I could tell that Dick wasn't thinking about his stock options, or the rest of his contract, or anything besides the red mist of his rage. I tried to throw him a lifeline. "You ought to talk to your counsel first, before doing anything rash," I said. "And we're not going to say anything to the press except, you know, something like 'he just doesn't get it.'"

Dick stormed out of the office, but not before turning back and uncorking one more, *Fuck you!*

We immediately put out a public statement about the dismissal, so I fielded some calls from the press.

A *Wall Street Journal* reporter, Meg Cox, called me and asked, "Okay, what's going on?"

I could have spilled the details. I could have told her about his refusal to work with the other Viacom divisions, the naked insubordination, the white-glove chauffeured limos, the commandeered elevators . . . the emperor. Instead, I stuck to my word and just told her, "All we're going to say is, *he just doesn't get it.*"

"Come on!" Meg wanted more dirt.

"Look, Meg, we've known each other a long time. That's as much as we're prepared to say."

It turns out that Meg would get the story anyway. Unbeknownst to me at the time, Dick had hired a PR guy, and the PR guy had contacted the *Wall Street Journal*, and he eventually arranged a lengthy meeting with Meg.

A few days later I received a call. Meg. "I owe you an apology," she said.

"For what?"

"Well, when you said, 'He doesn't get it,' I said no, no, there's *got* to be more to it than that."

"Right . . ."

"I was wrong," Meg said. "I just spent the afternoon with him. And he doesn't get it."

The next morning, the *Journal* printed a fairly rough story about Dick's departure.[9] The first line of the piece: "Richard Snyder still doesn't get it." The story covered all of his legendary accomplishments, and it also covered the reasons we needed to let him go, and how he "reigned by intimidation and fear over the publishing empire he built." The *Journal* noted, rightly, that this kind of departure was unheard of in Dick's thirty-three-year career. The *Journal* mentioned Philippe's involvement, and the story mentioned my involvement, but—as he had orchestrated—it barely mentioned Sumner.

Sumner had been worried that there would be call after call complaining about Dick's departure, and that the move would be radioactive.

9   Meg Cox and Johnnie L. Roberts, "Mergers & Manners: How the Despotic Boss of Simon & Schuster Found Himself Jobless—Snyder, Who Built Empire, Felt 'Business Is Conflict'; New Owners Disagreed—Dirty Words and Clean Soles," *Wall Street Journal*, Eastern edition, July 6, 1994, p. A1.

He was half right.

I did get about twenty phone calls, but they were roughly 19 to 1 in favor of, "I'm glad you finally got rid of him." I sensed vitriol from people he had dealt with in the past—perhaps ruthlessly, or even cruelly—and many had been waiting for this moment for a long time.

One of the only negative calls was from Bob Woodward, who had a relationship with Dick going back to the days of *All the President's Men*. He called and started to complain, and I quickly cut him off.

"Hey Bob, it's been a long time."

He paused for a second, and asked me what I meant.

"You don't remember my wife, Carol? Or Carol Oughton, as you knew her back then? We've met a few times."

"Oh, yeah, of course!"

The tension melted and we ended the call on friendly terms.

Another call was from Carly Simon. Most people know of her as a singer-songwriter (with hits like "You're So Vain," which, come to think of it, could apply to certain folks), but she's also the daughter of Richard Simon, the co-founder of Simon & Schuster. I happened to know Carly from mutual friends.

"Thank you, thank you," Carly said over the phone.

"What do you mean?"

Carly told me that years ago, when her kids were young, she had once been invited by Dick Snyder to the Simon & Schuster offices. Dick kept the kids waiting for an hour. When he finally appeared and gave the kids a tour, he did nothing but tell them how stupid their grandfather was for selling the place.

"I've just never forgiven it," she said. "I've been waiting years and years for this day."

Now wind the clock forward eighty-nine days after Dick's departure.

I got a call from my assistant. "You're not going to believe this," she said. "Dick Snyder's on the phone."

She was right—I was surprised. In our last conversation he had told me, on multiple occasions, that I should go fuck myself. Maybe he was calling to apologize?

"Put him through." A moment later. "Yes, Dick?"

"Well . . . I know this is a little awkward, but I need a favor," he said.

"Tell me what you need. If I can do it, we'll see what we can do."

"Well, it's been almost ninety days, and you know, my stock options are going to expire tomorrow."

I kept my voice neutral and calm. "Dick, I know you probably don't remember this conversation, but that's why we told you to get a lawyer. And we were happy to enter into a consulting agreement that would keep your options alive."

"Well, you know, it was the heat of the moment."

"I don't know what to tell you. My hands are tied," I said. And they were. There were four thousand other people from Paramount Communications in the same position, who had options about to expire. I've always tried to apply the same rules and principles to all employees equally, from top to bottom. This is just part of basic fairness. I explained this to him and said, "It's just not within my power to change it for one person."

I received a two-word response, and by now you can probably guess what those two words were.

After yelling those two words, he slammed the phone.

Simon & Schuster went on to do just fine without Dick Snyder.

It turns out that there was really only one person (besides Dick) who wasn't happy with the way things played out. Sumner Redstone was the one who had suggested that we get rid of Dick. When I asked him if he wanted to personally get involved, he had demurred. He hadn't wanted his fingerprints anywhere near it, worried that the press blowback would sully his reputation.

Yet there was no blowback. The press, in fact, seemed to approve. The day the *Journal* story came out, Sumner stormed into my office. "Why wasn't I in this story?"

"You didn't want to be in the story."

He fumed for a bit, upset that he hadn't gotten any credit.

Sumner Redstone liked getting the credit. At the time this was just a minor blip in our relationship, a hiccup in the early days of an otherwise smooth partnership. Yet this tick of his—the need to be in the story, the need to be *the* story—would eventually cost Viacom millions (perhaps billions) of dollars, and, ultimately, it would cost me my job.

Behind the Scenes

JANE

After Dad's passing, several people who knew what it was like to be empowered by Frank Biondi shared their stories with me. We first hear from Sherry Lansing (formerly of Paramount Pictures), then there is a story from Tom Freston, who was the frontline of a lot of groundbreaking original content development at MTV, and finally a tribute from Neil Braun, who says the best advice he ever got was from Dad.

Jade: No Apologies for Sound Decisions (by Sherry Lansing)

JANE

Sherry Lansing is the former chairman and CEO of Paramount Pictures; she ran the studio after it was acquired by Viacom and reported directly to Dad. "He ran it like a family," Sherry says. "We all knew we were important. We all knew that he cared about us." She explains that Dad helped create an atmosphere where "you're not afraid to fail," and that emboldened the creatives to take smart risks. Specifically, this one story stands out to her.

SHERRY

Early on in the Paramount and Viacom merger, we had *Forrest Gump* and *Clear and Present Danger*, so we were off to a good start. And then my husband Billy (William Friedkin), who's a very talented director, made a movie that Paramount distributed, called *Jade*.

Although *Jade* remains one of my favorite movies, unfortunately, it did not do well at the box office. And there I was, at the head of the studio. And I was releasing my husband's film. The first thing I thought was that I had let my husband down. Then I thought that I had let the studio down . . . and Frank, and Sumner Redstone, and Jon Dolgen. I really felt bad. It was more than just a feeling of disappointment—it was personal. All movies are personal, but this was really personal.

So the week after the release, I was in New York at the Viacom offices. I went and asked if I could see Frank. He said of course.

I came into his office, and I was feeling very emotional. I said to him, "I really want to apologize to you and tell you how sorry I am that the movie didn't work, and I'm really sorry that I let you down."

He looked at me. He had an almost amazed look on his face, and said, "What are you apologizing for? I love the movie. We love the movie. We're glad we made it. Sometimes it doesn't work out like you'd like it to. But you don't need to ever apologize."

And he meant it. Not everyone in the industry acts like that. Other people might say, "How could you let this happen?" But with Frank, there was nothing but kindness and understanding. I really believe you can tell a lot about people when they're successful, but you can tell even more about people when things aren't going well. Frank was always a gentleman, and always unflappable. Always so level. He was always there to support you.

Creation of Comedy Central (by Tom Freston)

JANE

There are endless stories about original content development by smart people that Dad hired. Here's one more. Know *The Daily Show, South Park, Broad City, Key & Peele*? All of these were hits on Comedy Central. And Comedy Central, in turn, can be traced back to my father's time at Viacom. This story also speaks to another attribute of my father's: the ability to be decisive. Once you've "done the work" and have gained (and earned) the confidence in your judgment, it's easier to make swift decisions. Tom Freston tells the story.

TOM

Frank paid attention to HBO, as they were a competitor and they had let him go. Michael Fuchs was running it at this point. He looked down on us like we were dirt, like we were some basic cable, local access channel.

Through the rumor mill, we had heard that Fuchs—who had made stand-up comedy a lynchpin at HBO, such as big specials from George Carlin and Billy Crystal—wanted to do a basic cable channel about comedy. They would take stand-up routines and chop them up into pieces. This would bring HBO into the basic cable business.

We knew that that would have been a logical move for HBO. Fuchs had all of these relationships with comedians, so that would have been a logical way for them to move into basic cable. So one day in early 1989, at my weekly staff meeting, someone slipped me a note that said, "HBO has just announced that they are going to launch this thing called The Comedy Channel."

This represented a real threat. We knew that if The Comedy Channel worked, and if they successfully entered the basic cable network game, then they would next launch a music channel, competing with MTV. So the most powerful company in the business would become our main competitor, whereas now we had the place to ourselves.

Instead we said, *We should announce a comedy channel.* I wanted to announce our own channel *today.* Because then we would be in every news story, and it would piss off Fuchs. (This was back in the seat-of-your-pants era of the cable and entertainment business, where things were really fun.)

So from this very staff meeting, I immediately called up Frank. I said, "Frank, I'm here with everybody, and your buddy Fuchs just announced this comedy channel. We want to announce a different one, and we're gonna call it Ha!'"

I pitched the idea of not just doing stand-up routines, but classic television shows and original comedic programming. I knew that it would ultimately cost a couple hundred million dollars before getting to breakeven.

There was no hesitation. Over the phone, Frank said, "Let's do it."

Can you imagine that? It was a hundred-million-dollar bet, and he loved it. And we were ultimately able to thwart HBO, because we would go to the cable operators who gave us distribution, and they'd say, *We don't want to piss off Viacom, and we don't want to piss off HBO,* so for two years *neither* of us really got any distribution.

But in the end, Fuchs gave up. And we merged, and it became Comedy Central, and it was a real victory for Frank. Comedy Central became a multibillion-dollar asset, and in the end, we bought out their half.

I view this as an example of Frank's willingness to take a shot from the gut on a big deal, with a deadline waving in front of him. If it didn't work, we could shut it down, but he thought, *Let's get into the game.*

The Best Advice I Ever Got (by Neil Braun)

Neil Braun, the former head of NBC Television and Viacom Entertainment, and dean emeritus of the Lubin School of Business at Pace University, was once a guest on the "Everyday MBA" podcast.[10] The host asked Neil to share the best advice he'd ever received. So he brought up my father.

Neil explained that he had twice been hired by my father: once when Dad ran HBO, and once when he ran Viacom. (Again, partnering for the long term.) After Neil's first year at Viacom, he sat down with my father for an informal performance review. Neil wanted to know how he was doing. Here's the rest of the story in Neil's words:

10 "STEM Education: Are Students Prepared?," Everyday MBA podcast, February 9, 2019, https://everydaymba.libsyn.com/stem-education-are-students-prepared.

NEIL

What Frank said to me kind of surprised me. He said, "You know, Neil, I really only care about two things. The first thing is trust, which has two dimensions. Integrity—and I've known you a long time . . . and I have no doubt about your integrity. And the second thing is judgment. And over time, I've seen you in lots of situations, and I've learned to trust your judgment."

Then Frank continued, "The second thing I care about is effectiveness. Whatever it is I ask you to do—whatever it is you say you're going to do—you get it done. I've decided a long time ago, the way to attract good people and keep good people is if I trust them, and they get it done, I really don't care about anything else."

I thought this was dead simple yet powerful advice and left his office pretty elated, thinking, *Wow*, how great it is to work for somebody who's going to manage me that way. Then I had an epiphany: *I wasn't managing my own staff that way*. So I adopted Frank's philosophy. From that day on, it completely changed how I managed people. It really was the singular best advice I've ever gotten, and it has profoundly affected not only how I manage, but how I think about all relationships.

The Frank Biondi Management Tree

JANE

Football fans are familiar with a concept called the "Bill Belichick Coaching Tree," where the legendary Patriots coach groomed and mentored an entire generation of young coaches, from Josh McDaniels to Nick Saban. Well, there's something of a "Frank Biondi Management Tree," as the list of executives he has managed and mentored is a Who's Who of Hollywood. As shown by the stories throughout this book, the tree includes Peter Chernin (the former head of 20th Century Fox, when it produced both *Titanic* and *Avatar*), Sherry Lansing (former CEO of Paramount Pictures), Jon Dolgen (former chairman of Viacom Entertainment Group), Tom Freston (later a CEO of Viacom), and Ken Solomon (CEO of The Tennis Channel).

Dad knew it all started with a strong team. "Hiring good people is really right at the top," he said, and then he trusted them to do what they're good at. "Make sure your people have access to resources, whether that's capital or training programs or you name it," he added. This skill becomes increasingly important as you move up the ranks, and perhaps essential as the scope of the organization widens, as it did at Viacom when they acquired Blockbuster and Paramount.

And just as important: treat that team with respect. "I always try to treat the people I work with—whether they reported to me on the org chart, or were above me, or peers—as colleagues," he explained. "You get an awful lot out of people when you treat them as an equal."

Dad also knew how to use a sense of humor to lighten the mood, from the frequent dry quips to the occasional sly practical joke. Just ask Henry Schleiff, whom my father had hired at both HBO and Viacom.

When Viacom moved their corporate headquarters to 1515 Broadway to consolidate the divisions, my father was in charge of overseeing the move. Some of the division heads lobbied for their own private bathrooms, including Henry, who as Dad put it, was being "unbelievably persistent." So after construction was finished, and when the executives moved into their shiny new digs, Henry entered his corporate office to discover his own private bathroom . . . in the form of a urinal glued to the wall. My father had asked the construction guys to install the urinal over the weekend; for Henry, alas, there was no plumbing attached. (Henry was a good sport and loves this story.)

Humor aside, Viacom even won an Emmy for one of Nickelodeon's original content series, *Rugrats*. The creative team actually gave their Emmy award to my father, because without his investment and belief in what they set out to build, the show never would have happened.

He had that Emmy on his desk until the day he died.

CHAPTER 7

Substance vs. Sizzle

We live in an era that's obsessed with image. Just look at our fascination with Instagram, TikTok, and the rest of social media.

And while the world at large is infatuated with glitz, the media industry takes it to a comically exaggerated level. Red carpet events. Selfies with Kardashians. Flattering headlines in TMZ or *Variety*. But even with his chosen industry's lure of fame, my father never cared about the sizzle. He was all substance.

"Being willing to accomplish what you want to accomplish, and letting the other person be on the red carpet, was what Frank was all about," says Alan Schwartz, former CEO of Bear Stearns. He adds that some people are fueled by a sense of inner accomplishment, and some people are driven by a sense of outer accomplishment. "Frank was one of those guys that had an inner sense of accomplishment."

Sherry Lansing, former chair and CEO of Paramount, agrees. "The flash didn't interest him," she says. "You can tell a lot about a person by the people who are at their birthdays year after year. If it's a different crop of people every year, you know that that person doesn't really have good values, because they're trading their friends in, based on success or failure. Frank had the same friends his whole life. He liked who he liked, and he kept his friends forever."

Whether it was choosing the right discount rate, rummaging through the accounting footnotes, or negotiating fairly to build a fruitful partnership, my father focused on the things he best understood and could control. Just as he flanked himself with the best possible team, he believed that the work and its outcomes were what mattered most, not the headlines.

"He created a culture that was not of flash. We were all about the work. That was all that was important," says Sherry, of the culture he created at Viacom and Paramount. She views this culture that was nurtured by my father—and Jon Dolgen (who reported to Dad, and then Sherry reported to Jon)—as a key reason for the '90s-era success of Paramount Studios, which included hits that ranged from *Braveheart* to *Mission: Impossible* to *Tommy Boy*.

Yet the way this played out in my father's career was a little more nuanced. The media industry *does* care about sizzle, and Dad might have lost some points for shrugging off the glitz. After work, many Hollywood executives would head out to a celebrity-packed see-and-be-seen restaurant . . . and Dad would head home to have dinner with Mom and my sister and me. But those were his values. He lived on his own terms, comfortable with who he was.

Ultimately, this quiet self-confidence earned the respect of others. As Alan Schwartz explains, many of the celebrities and titans of industry are accustomed to people acting one of two ways around them: 1) sycophantic, which loses their respect; or 2) trying to prove that they're better, which can be off-putting. My father didn't fall into that trap. "Frank, on the one hand, he didn't kiss up to them, but on the other, he didn't challenge them or try and prove he was better," said Alan. "And all of a sudden, they wanted him to respect *them*. Because they didn't understand how he could be so anchored around his inner sense of accomplishment."

Many are drawn to the movie business because of the glitz and the glamour—not just actors dreaming of Hollywood fame, but also the suits behind the scenes. Take my father's most prominent and showy boss, Sumner Redstone. Sumner had bright orange hair that was almost Trumpian. He had a thick Boston accent. One night Sumner was caught in a hotel fire. He hung from a third-floor windowsill by his right hand, waiting to be rescued. His hand was badly burned for the rest of his life, to the point where he strapped his tennis racket to his hand because he couldn't move his fingers.

This is all to say that Sumner Redstone, an outsized character, wanted to be a movie *mogul*. His entertainment industry career began when he began working at his father's movie theater chain, National Amusements, and from then on he was enamored by the movie studios and the stars. He thirsted for that movie spotlight so much that he would pursue buying Viacom and, ultimately, Paramount to fulfill his personal dream. He was drawn to the sizzle.

And it wasn't just Redstone. My father worked alongside plenty of executives who cared more about their own press than the substance of the work. And by "press" I mean this literally. To illustrate that point, Dad liked to share a story about one of his closest colleagues at HBO. A *Wall Street Journal* reporter once gave Dad a courtesy "heads up" call about a profile they were writing about this executive, and she told Dad: "We've interviewed quite a few people, and let's just say the conclusion is that he is somewhere between a major jerk and a total ass. There is one more interview with the main reporter on Thursday. And if he declines to do it, then the article won't run."

My father was grateful for the tip. He told his colleague not to do the next interview, which would kill the story and save him from embarrassment. Amazingly, the colleague went ahead with the interview, the story ran, and Dad learned about it in the paper. "I figured the reporter was a woman, and I could just charm her into changing her opinion," the colleague told him. Dad couldn't understand or relate. And that's what happens when you care more about sizzle than substance.

He taught me that there are many ways to define achievement, but that too often we let others, or society, do most of the defining (the sizzle); it's important that you craft your own sense of purpose (the substance).

In this chapter, my father shares some stories that touch on the themes of substance and sizzle, many from his time working for Redstone. One of the stories, about a rare public acknowledgment of my father's contributions to Viacom—a lengthy profile in *The New Yorker* titled "Redstone's Secret Weapon"—is what led Sumner to fire him. I can still remember where I was when I read it, at boarding school in my American History classroom, waiting for class to start. Dad was never bitter about it. Instead he just pointed to the life-changing opportunity Redstone gave him to run the company.

My father had a great sense of humor about the hazards that came with working for billionaire owners, Redstone being the most notable. In the early nineties, before he left Viacom, one of his friends, an owner of a Major League Baseball team, had asked Dad casually (not formally) if he would consider the opportunity to be commissioner of Major League Baseball. Dad's response that he always recalled with a chuckle and a twinkle in his eye: "I already have one incorrigible billionaire boss, I don't need thirty."

Sizzle Wins Out: The NBC Deal That Wasn't

JANE

This is a little-known story that could have had massive implications to the media industry. In the early '90s, my father nearly orchestrated the purchase of NBC . . . until one voice intervened at the last moment.

FRANK

By 1992, it was apparent to all of us in the management group at Viacom, including Sumner Redstone, that we had sufficiently turned around the businesses. We had successfully recapitalized the company.

The MTV Networks had a clear runway for future growth. So we looked for other ways to expand—maybe through an acquisition?

We concluded that we had enough market cap—and enough borrowing power—that we could acquire at least one other substantial media operation. We scoured the landscape for logical candidates.

It turns out that Sumner had a relationship with Martin Davis, the chief executive of Paramount Communications. This included Paramount Studios, Simon & Schuster, and Madison Square Garden. Sumner thought that Paramount would be an ideal target (more on that later).

The talks with Marty Davis didn't go anywhere, negotiations broke down, so we continued our exploration for other media acquisitions.

Several months later, we were contacted by bankers for General Electric (GE), saying that they had decided they were going to sell NBC . . . but with one condition: The buyer must pay at least what General Electric had paid for NBC several years earlier—$3.8 billion.

We agreed that we'd go up to GE's headquarters in Connecticut and do some due diligence. Viacom's senior management team, the general counsel, and I made the trip. We paid a courtesy call to Jack Welch, and then we settled in with GE's chief financial officer, who gave us a data dump of the company's operations.

The state of play at the time: NBC the network was marginally losing money; the TV station group was reasonably profitable; and the two cable networks, MSNBC and CNBC, were doing quite nicely—but they were a small, very small part of the operations.

We knew that $3.8 billion was quite a price tag. This was a fairly hefty multiple of the profit that NBC earned each year. So we scratched our heads as to how this could make sense. We asked them for a breakdown of each division. They said the station group was worth $2.9 billion, the NBC network was worth $500 million, and the two cable networks (CNBC and MSNBC) made up the balance, around $350 million.

After talking it through, we concluded that the only assets that looked reasonably priced were NBC the network ($500 million) and the cable networks (a bargain at $350 million). So Tom Dooley, our chief financial officer, said to GE's CFO, "I know you guys are bound and determined to get $3.8 billion, and you don't want to take a loss. But would you consider breaking the deal up into pieces?"

Tom continued: "Would you keep the stations, if we gave you the longest affiliation agreement that the FCC would agree to? And then we buy the network for $500 million, and the cable networks for $350 million?"

The CFO thought for a minute. "Interesting," he said. "It's kind of above my pay grade. Let me ask, and I'll get back to you."

He left the room, and then came back in about thirty minutes. "We'd sell the NBC network, and we'd also sell the cable networks for a total of $850 million."

We couldn't believe it. This deal was mind-bogglingly attractive. We ballparked the cable networks to be worth much, much more than the $350 million that GE was asking—and when you flash forward in time, the growth of MSNBC and CNBC proved that to be true.

But back in GE headquarters, we played it cool. We didn't want to show any overt enthusiasm. "Hey, let us get back to New York and sit down with Redstone, and we'll get back to you pretty quickly with an answer," we told the CFO. He agreed. It looked like NBC would be ours.

On the drive back to New York, the car brimmed with excitement. We had stumbled into an incredibly attractive transaction, and we knew it. We called Redstone to share the good news.

"Hold on, hold on," Sumner said over the car phone. "Forget about NBC. I don't care what the deal is."

Wait. What?

"I just got a call from Martin Davis," Sumner continued, "and he wants to reopen the Paramount conversations." Sumner was giddy. He loved the idea of being a movie mogul, and he loved the idea of owning Paramount.

Sumner always had a soft spot for that studio. Much earlier in his career, when Sumner first started in the drive-in movie business, and when he was still just small potatoes, Paramount was the only studio that would take a meeting with him. For him, the lure of Paramount was irresistible. It was both sentiment and sizzle that drew him in.

"But we just had this unbelievable meeting with NBC and GE," I told him.

Screw that, he basically said. *We're not doing that; we're doing Paramount.*

We passed on the NBC deal, most of us quite reluctantly. But there wasn't much you could say when the owner of your company was so dead-set on catching his white whale . . . and thus the Paramount negotiations began.

JANE

I was only a teenager at the time, but I remember the drama of these high-stakes negotiations, of Dad leaving in the early mornings for daily meetings and the escalating bids requiring that they find partners to help finance the deal. Dad had planned to take me to Lillehammer, Norway, for the 1994 Olympic Games that winter, as NYNEX (the telephone company that became Verizon) was a sponsor of the U.S. Olympic team, and had invited him and a guest. He had to cancel the trip as this deal heated up. I was disappointed. I had never been to Europe and had renewed my passport in anticipation. But I understood the pressure he was under, and how important it was for Viacom. He took me out to dinner instead, just the two of us. I forget where we went, but will never forget the gesture.

Still Blinded by the Sizzle: The Battle for Paramount

FRANK

So NBC was out, and Paramount was back in play.

I was not particularly in favor of this deal, because it had a hefty price tag. But Sumner was adamant.

And by 1993, the financials of Viacom had truly turned around. When Sumner acquired the company in 1987 and when I took the reins as CEO, Viacom's stock traded in the low teens. And when the market crashed in '87, it traded in the mid–single digits. Then it climbed back up. By 1993 it was in the mid-60s, which let us think about acquisitions such as NBC or Paramount.

A few months before the potential NBC deal, Sumner had talked with Martin Davis, then the head of Paramount, about a friendly merger. They retained an investment banker (Herbert Allen, of Allen & Company) to mediate the exchange ratio between the two companies, but they couldn't agree on a ratio. That fell apart.

Now what we didn't know, and what Sumner didn't know, but what Martin Davis *did* know, is that a new suitor for Paramount had entered the frame: Barry Diller, who was then the head of QVC, the home shopping network.

Barry Diller had deep roots at Paramount. He had run the studio for a decade, from 1974 to 1984. Under his watch, Paramount cranked out hit after hit, including *Raiders of the Lost Ark*, *Grease*, *Beverly Hills Cop*, and TV staples like *Taxi* and *Cheers*. But that was then. Diller had lost his job when Martin Davis fired him, and now the two were rivals.

This was one of the more notable "parting of ways" in corporate history. Given their bad blood, Davis was quite anxious to avoid being taken over by QVC and his arch-rival, Barry Diller. And Diller wasn't looking for a friendly merger: he threatened a hostile takeover. So just as Martin Davis caught wind of Diller's plan, and as we were driving back from the NBC meeting, the Viacom and Paramount conversations resumed.

Here was Sumner's thought at the time: Viacom and Paramount would work out a friendly merger, hammer out a stock exchange ratio that both sides could agree upon, Sumner would remain chairman, with Martin Davis as president and CEO. This would have meant a demotion for me—I was then the CEO, and the change would be both Stanley Jaffe and I would become chief operating officers.

I wasn't prepared to quit over this, and it was early in the game, so I agreed to it. But before we could ever get there, Barry Diller jumped in and triggered a bidding war between Viacom and QVC, escalating the price for Paramount.

The bidding war lasted for months. Each time, the deal got more expensive, and the price soared from an original offer of mid-$60s per share to approximately $100 per share. The negotiations were tense. Every morning at seven a.m., I would go to the Burlington Building on Sixth Avenue, up to the Smith Barney offices.

As the cost of the deal increased, we soon needed more partners to raise our investment. So we joined forces first with NYNEX (now Verizon), who chipped in $1.2 billion, then with Blockbuster, who added $600 million.

We made what we felt would be our last and final bid, and then even *that* was topped by Diller and QVC. We had reached a Catch-22: Every time we increased the price of our bid (in terms of dollar per share of stock), the value of our stock would go down . . . which lowered the effective bid. Translation? At a certain point we could no longer offer just more stock, but needed to offer more cash.

And we didn't have any more cash. So we put our heads together, along with the heads of NYNEX (Verizon) and Blockbuster, to try and figure out a solution. But at this point, honestly, most of us were resigned to losing Paramount. Our stock price had plunged from the $60s to the $20s, which seemed to doom our bid.

So I said, somewhat jokingly, "Listen, the only way we can make this work is if we can find someone who would buy a security that pegged the Viacom price in the mid-60s, even though it's trading in the high 20s."

To everyone's surprise, someone spoke up and said, "Hey, I would do that."

The voice belonged to Wayne Huizenga, the head of Blockbuster and co-owner of the Miami Dolphins. "With one condition," Wayne continued. He said that regardless of whether we were successful in getting Paramount, in the aftermath, Viacom would unconditionally merge with Blockbuster, at a fixed exchange rate.

So we had a deal.

What we didn't realize at the time, but which became quickly apparent after we had struck a merger with Blockbuster, was that Wayne had calculated that, as a board member, he could vote *against* the Paramount merger, effectively preventing Viacom from being successful. This (in his theory) would drive the price of Viacom stock up from the mid-$20s to something north of $50, and with his fixed exchange rate, he—and other shareholders in Blockbuster—would reap a loftier purchase price than what we at Viacom had thought we had negotiated.

In other words, for several months, Viacom's price had been tanking *because of the merger talks*, from the $60s to the $20s. Wayne was confident that the price would recover from the $20s to where it had been originally—*if he personally scuttled the Paramount deal*, even though we only made the deal with him for the express purpose of acquiring Paramount. This looked like foul play. It felt like foul play.

So the board convened to vote on the Paramount bid, and the mood was tense. Wayne had the power to scrap the deal. Through his lawyer, Redstone basically said to Wayne, "Look, I'm not happy with the position you're taking. But I've got to tell you, you're exposing yourself to all sorts of personal liability by taking this position. I'm confident that if you consult with your counsel, they will agree that it's a perilous route that you're trying to travel and that you should turn your vote to the affirmative."

Wayne agreed to speak with his legal counsel. The board took a break, he huddled with his attorneys, and we all returned a few hours later.

Somewhat chagrined, Wayne said that his lawyers essentially agreed with the legal argument that Sumner had put forth, and that he would vote for the Paramount merger.

The deal went through. History can debate whether the acquisition made sense, as it did give us a trove of new assets (Simon & Schuster, Madison Square Garden, and of course Paramount and Blockbuster), but also a staggering load of debt—the deal ultimately cost $10 billion—that loomed for years, and eventually caused us to divest some of those assets, like Madison Square Garden. We were fortunate that one of Paramount's first pictures after the deal ended up doing okay: *Forrest Gump*. And while everyone understood that Blockbuster Video would eventually be phased out by digital, it still offered substantial short-term growth. (Back in 1994, Netflix streaming was still over a decade away.)

At the time of the deal, and after the bruising months of negotiations, in early 1994, Barry Diller issued a simple statement: "They won, we lost, next."

My Departure from Viacom

JANE

It seems that eventually the fundamental difference between Dad and Sumner, substance vs. sizzle, led to an untenable situation. Here's how Dad recounts what happened when he left Viacom.

FRANK

As 1995 rolled on, it became quite apparent that Sumner Redstone was unhappy with my continued presence at Viacom. From the small and petty, to maybe the more important, things began to change. For example, our public relations people told me that they were under orders from Sumner to make sure that I never got an interview, particularly one that would feature me on the cover of a magazine, or with a photograph. In another example, in 1995 the annual Christmas party, which my wife and I had hosted for years, was suddenly being hosted by Sumner.

So as the year turned over into early 1996, Sumner asked if he could come in and talk about the future.

I said sure.

He came into my office and closed the door, which was atypical for him. You could tell from his body language he was quite uncomfortable.

"Look, it's been terrific working together," he said, "but I've made my mind up. It's time for you to move on."

"Really?" I said. I mean, the business was good. It wasn't *great*, as the Paramount deal wasn't quite working out as Sumner had hoped, but there were encouraging signs. "It's your company," I told him. "You can do what you want. But I think you're making a big mistake."

"It's simply . . . I'm tired," he said. "I've been here a long time. When I got here, I really didn't know the businesses that well. You carried us through. And now I feel like I understand the businesses. And quite honestly, I'm tired of sharing the credit."

A pause.

"I promise you I'll honor your contract," he said. And he did.

So we moved on. I left the company, and shortly thereafter I joined Universal Studios as chief executive officer.

And in many respects, I think this was the end of the glory years of Viacom—where it had rebounded from a B-class citizen in the media world, to a strong, much-admired, well-managed (and I don't necessarily mean *by me* well-managed; we had an excellent team) group of individuals. From that point on, the philosophies began to change.

Shortly thereafter, Viacom merged with CBS, giving out a substantial amount of stock, which inhibited the price performance, as the underlying various divisions didn't live up to expectations. And it started a slow, steady migration of managers out of Viacom to other posts in the media industry, representing a sizable brain drain.

Now, nearly a quarter-century after I was fired, Viacom is desperately trying to rebuild its businesses, which had been long underinvested after my departure, in favor of buying back stock . . . most of which had been issued in the CBS acquisition.

At this point for me, it's neither here nor there. I don't own Viacom stock anymore. But it really is sort of sad and wistful, to see what was once a strong management group and a strong business withered down to a mere shadow of its former self.

As for the day Sumner fired me? The odd thing is that it came only a couple of days after a lavish celebratory dinner we shared—toasting the success of some premiere—with our wives and a couple of other senior execs. That night we were on top of the world. And then, a few days later: boom.

On the fateful day itself, after Sumner left my office, I called my wife, Carol. She knew that I was scheduled to go to China, to speak at a Lehman Brothers conference. This would have been a fun trip, and she was looking forward to joining me.

I called Carol and said, "I've got some good news and bad news."

"Well, okay, what's the bad news?"

"The bad news is we're not going to China," I said. "And that's because of the good news. Sumner just fired me."

She just laughed and said, "I'm putting a bottle of champagne in the fridge. I'll see you when you get home."

The Sumner-Biondi Dynamic

JANE

Was there more to the story of why Sumner asked my father to leave Viacom? I can't help but wonder if Dad's focus on substance over sizzle created a fundamental rift between the two of them.

For some perspective and context, I spoke again with Tom Freston. As the head of MTV Networks, Tom had a front-row seat to the evolution of my father and Sumner's relationship. "They got off to a good start," remembers Tom. "Frank made a lot of good, smart early moves." And when Sumner first took over Viacom, as Tom puts it,

"Sumner didn't know his ass from his elbow." So in the first few years, my father effectively played the part of mentor.

"I was impressed, in the early days, of the deference Sumner gave to Frank," says Tom. "Frank really called the shots. Sumner was an apprentice, in a way. He was listening to everybody, seeing how the deals went down, seeing what the issues were, and he had a mind like a trap."

Just one specific example: My father held a staff meeting every Tuesday morning at ten a.m. All of the senior executives, seated around the table, took turns giving updates. "Frank would sit at the head of the table, not Sumner," remembers Tom. "Sumner would basically sit there and not say a peep. He didn't bring a pad of paper. He didn't bring anything. He just had a phone sitting by his side, because he was obsessed with the stock price. So he would tell his broker throughout the day to 'buy buy buy' or 'sell sell sell.'"

As the years ticked by, and as Viacom grew and became more profitable, three things happened: My father began to get some credit for his success, Sumner learned the business, and Sumner began to get resentful. "I think Sumner began to gradually think that 'my apprenticeship is over, and I'm going to step out, and I can be the CEO of this company,'" says Tom. "You know, I think Sumner had a lot of traits that really remind me of Donald Trump. Kind of a blowhard. A narcissist. He had a sense of megalomania that I didn't notice at first, that really grew over time."

Redstone wanted more credit, more spotlight, more sizzle. "He would get jealous of Frank, because we were making good moves, and the company was moving up," says Tom. "The company was sort of moving up in the ranks, and Frank was getting credit for that. Although Frank was the last guy to go out and take bows for stuff. He really let other people take the glory. He was great like that. He was not an egotist at all."

Then came *The New Yorker* article. In late 1994, one of the magazine's senior media writers, Ken Auletta, shadowed my father for two months for a deeply reported, thirteen-thousand-word profile of him called "Redstone's Secret Weapon." For perspective, thirteen thousand words is about one-fifth of the length of this book. The article was published in January 1995. Auletta noted that my father "travels just beneath the public radar" but that he is the one who calls the shots.

"Redstone bought Viacom, but Biondi is the one who has built it," Auletta wrote. "It is Biondi to whom other Viacom executives come for day-to-day decisions, Biondi who tells them when they have strayed from their budget plan, Biondi who fires people, and Biondi who presides over the monthly meetings of the company's key managers."

The article did not sit well with Sumner. The glowing profile was "the crowning blow," remembers Tom, as it inflamed Sumner's jealousy. "There was nothing untruthful" about the article, says Tom, "but I think that really bugged Sumner. Because Frank got fired soon thereafter. Sumner decided, 'I'm going to do this. I don't need Frank Biondi anymore.'"

And there was one odd—and telling—coda to the departure: Sumner did something quite unusual; he chose to enforce the non-compete clause in my father's contract. Usually when you fire someone you would be indifferent to their next job choice, even if it's with a competitor. But Sumner knew what my father was capable of, as he had proven it at Viacom. It was clear to everyone paying attention that he was not terminated for performance reasons. The situation became a running joke; Dad's financial advisor even printed a T-shirt with my father's picture on it saying "Free Frank Biondi."

Of course, all of this put my father in some good company. "When Sumner gets you on his radar screen and you start bugging him, sooner or later you get fired," says Tom, who later ran Viacom. "He fired me for not buying MySpace."

Dodging the Misses: The *Star Wars* Heart Attack

JANE

Dad was never shy when it came to pushing the boundaries to make a deal. But he always had a firm grasp on reality, drew a firm line, and he stuck to his guns . . . even if his counterparties were George Lucas or Steven Spielberg.

FRANK

When you think of HBO, you probably think of the hits like *Game of Thrones* or *Sex and the City*. Yet during my years there (1978–1984) and far from the celebrities and the Emmys and the spotlight, there was a very different game being played.

What most people don't realize is that HBO's foundational growth—and profits—came from tough negotiations, clever use of data (covered earlier), a respect for the budget, and even the occasional heart attack.

Just ask George Lucas, or maybe Steven Spielberg. From 1977 to the mid-'80s, HBO was almost religious about driving down its content costs. We were sticklers.

Yet we also wanted the blockbuster movies. HBO's bread and butter has always been movies. That was true in the '80s and it's still true today. The key to growth, we knew, was to offer more feature films than the competition. We gobbled up market share through superior content, just like Netflix does today. These two conflicting values—a desire for the best content, and a push to curb the costs—came to a head in 1981, when 20th Century Fox tried to sell us the rights to broadcast *Star Wars*.

The Fox execs, led by Steve Roberts and his number two, Larry, paid us a visit at HBO headquarters in New York. The room was filled with a handful of Fox execs, a handful of HBO execs, and a tinge of cigar smoke—courtesy of our cigar-loving head of film acquisition, Steve Scheffer, who was, at that point, the largest buyer of film in the world.

Steve and Larry gave Fox's pitch. "*Star Wars* is one of a kind," he said. "It's going to change the landscape of television." *Star Wars* was such a hit that Fox had waited a few years after the theatrical release (1977) to offer it to HBO; usually that happened within a year. He rattled off all the platitudes you might expect about what was then the top-grossing film of all time: *Extraordinary, the biggest ever, game-changer.*

We politely listened to the wind-up. And we knew that, to some extent, he was correct. *Star Wars* was an undisputed phenomenon, and clearly it belonged in our lineup. Yet we also had a budget. We honored those budgets. Our rule of thumb was to pay studios 25 to 50 cents per subscriber, and at the time we had around ten million subscribers, so that meant $2.5 to $5 million. We also demanded exclusivity. (If a movie aired on HBO, you couldn't find it on Showtime or CBS.) What would *Star Wars* ask for?

"$4 per subscriber," the Fox negotiator said. "And no exclusivity."

Or $40 million. Or eight times more than we had ever paid.

It's true that we coveted *Star Wars*, **but not even The Force can overcome The Math.**

It's easy to let the power of celebrity cloud your judgment, but if something is too expensive to cost-justify, you have to draw a line. Have the confidence to say no. Sure, out of consideration of *Star Wars'* unique stature, we could maybe—*maybe*—go to $1, but if we buckled to a demand as high as $4 per sub, then we would lose money and, worse, set a dangerous precedent, which might cost us leverage in future deals.

The room was silent. The Fox executives, anxious, looked at us for a response.

Finally, Steve (from HBO) said, with a twinkle in his eye, "Guys, I love everything you say, and we'd be perfectly happy to pay you 50 cents a subscriber."

Larry's face went white. He clutched his chest. And he had a heart attack.

He literally had a heart attack, collapsing in his chair.

Thus ended the first round of negotiations.

Larry would be fine, thank God. We called for medical attention, the paramedics arrived within minutes, and Larry would make a full recovery.

The deal recovered too. In the end, both sides made concessions; we (grudgingly) punted on exclusivity, and they (grudgingly) slashed their price to $1 per subscriber, which bent—but did not break—our budget.

The heart attack, in a sense, only solidified our reputation as hard-ass negotiators. Whether your industry is the movies or tech or finance or plumbing, it's likely that you will, at some point, negotiate with the "big names" of the space. You can't be swayed or cowed by that star power.

Another example: a few years later, our negotiating mettle would once again be tested by an A-lister with heat, this time from Universal.

"We've got a really unique proposition for you," my Universal contact said on the phone.

"What would that be?"

"I can't say just yet. But it's going to knock your socks off."

Cryptically, Universal insisted that they could only share this incredible idea in person, so they came to our offices and gave us the pitch: Steven Spielberg comes to HBO.

That almost happened. In a parallel universe, we say yes to the deal and Spielberg is part of the HBO family. At the time the idea was unprecedented. Nowadays you have David Fincher (*Mindhunter*) and Steven Soderbergh (*The Knick*) and even Martin Scorsese (*Boardwalk Empire*) dabbling in prestige TV, but in the '80s, it was unheard of for an A-list director to sully their hands with television. Besides, this was Steven Spielberg! Peak Spielberg! He still basked in the glow of *Jaws* and *Raiders* and *E.T.*

The hottest director on the planet had just committed to helming *Amazing Stories*, an updated take on *The Twilight Zone*.

"This is Steven Spielberg," they said. "This is going to make all the difference in the world."

Who could possibly say no?

The one catch, and there's always a catch, is that Universal wanted $1 million an episode. At the time, we only spent a fraction of that; our original programming was still stand-up specials and music concerts. "We'll put our heads together and get back to you," I said.

At almost every point of my career, at the core, my job was to estimate value. So how do you value an opportunity like this? Yes, it's true that the name Spielberg has cachet, and it would bring some intangible benefits. But with a twenty-episode season (standard back in the '80s), that meant a $20 million price tag, and at the time, HBO as a whole was only making $100 million in profit.

On the other hand, surely there was value to the sizzle factor, the Spielberg mojo. In theory, a hit show would help us grow our subscriber base. Yet we were already growing. We were growing at a rapid clip. Even if *Amazing Stories* was as successful as the Universal execs would like us to believe, would that lead to *incremental* growth above and beyond our current trajectory? The math didn't add up. Even a hit show would prove costly. (A more recent example: One quiet reason for *Game of Thrones'* shortened seasons is that even though it was a hit, the cost of the late-season contracts became tough to cost-justify.)

This is why our head of programming told them, "Sorry, we appreciate the offer, but it's not for us."

Universal was floored. They shopped it around to other networks, and they eventually sold *Amazing Stories* to NBC. To great hype and fanfare, Steven Spielberg directed the pilot episode. To somewhat less fanfare, because of low ratings and a princely budget, NBC canceled the show after two seasons.

The hits get all the glory, but sometimes it's just as important to dodge the misses.

EBIDTA vs. Sizzle (by Greg Meidel)

JANE

To end this chapter about substance and sizzle, I turned to one of Dad's close friends, thirty-year tennis partner, and former direct report, Greg Meidel, who was then the CEO of Universal Television Group. Greg also oversaw Universal's international television. This story involves an Emmy won by *Law & Order*. Here's what Greg told me:

GREG

In 1997, *Law & Order* won an Emmy for the first time. That was a Sunday night. I stayed out a little too late celebrating with Dick Wolf after we won, and let's just say I was a little slow the next morning.

Monday morning was a staff meeting with Frank and Ron Meyer [COO of Universal Studios], like usual. I was a bit late to the meeting. I came into the staff meeting and proudly carried the trophy. "We just won an Emmy!" I nearly shouted, hoisting the award. "This is huge!"

Frank just looked at me like I was from Pluto. There was zero emotion, no excitement. He looked at me for maybe thirty seconds.

"What does that mean for your numbers?" he asked me. "What's the financial impact of this?" And he drilled me with more questions.

It was classic Frank. He's always thinking about strategic planning, and about the impact to things like revenue and profits and cash flows. He brought everything back to the importance of EBITDA: earnings before interest, taxes, depreciation, and amortization. Prior to working for Frank, this was not something I necessarily focused on. He taught me to love EBITDA. Frank knows that it's a glamorous business, but at the end of the day it's just like any other business. Grow your revenue. Reduce your costs. So two weeks after that post-Emmy's Monday staff meeting, in honor of Frank, I went to the DMV. And I ordered a custom license plate: EBITDA.

That license plate is on my car to this day.

CHAPTER 8

Know Your Value(s)

Spreadsheets and philosophy have more in common than you'd think.

"Know your value(s)" works on two different levels: 1) Understand your values, principles, and what counts as success; 2) Know how to estimate the value of things. Value can take many forms: the value of companies, the value of partnerships, the value of your contributions at work.

One ability in business that's often overlooked is the knack for understanding value. My father was good at this. He was *great* at this. He excelled at every type of value analysis. If his corporation was considering a major acquisition? Then he could crunch the numbers and figure out what it was worth. (As was the case with Embassy, Merv Griffin Enterprises, Castle Rock, and Paramount.) He realized—decades ahead of most—that the real value in media was original content, so he worked again and again to deliver that to consumers.

In rereading his wisdom while assembling this book—and now that he is gone—it is even clearer to me that he had a particular skill in assessing what mattered, assessing value, the substance of what made something special or distinguished. He could clearly identify why something worked as a business, or was satisfying to him personally or professionally, and help others do the same.

In the stories in this chapter, he recounts a few such analyses of what mattered to him, and also a few examples of where others let personal fixation cloud their judgment.

The Value of the Job Offer

JANE

As my father told me many times, the media industry is a small world. You run into the same players again and again. So maybe it shouldn't be surprising that a key figure during my father's time at Viacom—Barry Diller, in the battle for Paramount—would, years earlier, have given him some career advice that he would never forget.

FRANK

One morning, when I was the CEO of HBO, my office phone rang. I picked it up.

"This is Ted Ashley," said the voice on the other end. Ted was a legend in the entertainment business—the chairman of Warner Bros. film studio for over a decade, and then serving at the time as vice chairman of Warner Communications. This is not a phone call you ignore.

"You know, we own The Movie Channel," Ted said on the call, which of course I did know. In fact, it was jointly owned by Warner, Universal, and Paramount and would later be consolidated with Showtime when its owner, Viacom, joined the venture. "We want to make some changes," he said. "And we'd really like to talk to you about coming over as CEO." More specifically, he explained, as the CEO of Showtime and The Movie Channel.

This was a flattering proposal, but I already had a job as CEO of HBO, and this was a job I enjoyed.

"Look, it sounds like a long shot," I said, as The Movie Channel and Showtime were in a distant second and third place to HBO, and not growing at nearly the same clip.

Ted was undeterred. "Well if you're open for a conversation, let me see if I can find a date for breakfast here in New York, with the folks from Warner Communications and Paramount and Universal."

So about a month later, sure enough, we met for breakfast along with Sid Sheinberg from Universal and Barry Diller, at the time from Paramount. Both were titans. Sidney Sheinberg ran Universal for decades, and in 1968, he gave the first big break to a promising young director named Steven Spielberg.

They pitched me on what they thought could be done with The Movie Channel and Showtime, suggesting new formats and programming. But I guess it was obvious that I wasn't entirely sold by their presentation. It was clear that I had some doubts, despite the massive potential bump in pay. (I was grateful for my salary, but HBO lived in the Time Inc. universe—HBO was a subsidiary—so the executives weren't as well compensated as others in the entertainment industry.)

Then the conversation took a turn.

Barry Diller, who I did not know very well at that point, in his distinct style, cut in and said, "Look, you seem a bit torn."

That was fair. I was. Diller continued, "If you're really talking to us about this job because it pays a million dollars, as opposed to because it's an interesting, unique opportunity . . . then I would just say 'thanks,' and leave. Because if I'm willing to pay you a million dollars, then a lot of other people are going to be willing to pay you a million dollars. So that shouldn't really figure into your calculus."

"Okay," I said. "Fair enough. Good advice. Let me mull on it and get back to you."

We broke up the breakfast on a relatively cordial note, and I ultimately got back to them and said, "I appreciate the offer, but I'm going to pass."

This was a lesson that I forever took to heart. It's important to know the value of money in a job offer, but then balance that against the opportunity, challenges, and inherent rewards of the job itself.

The Hasbro and DreamWorks Deal That Never Was

JANE

My father sat on over twenty boards over the course of his career. One of them was The Tennis Channel, where, as CEO and chairman Ken Solomon remembers, "We always looked to Frank. At the end of every board meeting, there would have been lots of debate, and Frank would sit there quietly and listen, and finally we would turn to him as if to say, 'What do you think?' He would synthesize everything. And he had this incredible judgment." So maybe it's no surprise that Dad helped Hasbro avoid making a $3 billion mistake in how to value a company, as he shares in this story.

FRANK

As of 2014, I had been on the Hasbro board for over a decade, since 2002. I watched as the company had turned itself around—masterfully—from losing money to growing into a real juggernaut, with $1 billion in profit. It clearly surpassed its rival, Mattel. (And the industry had come a long way from the days of Topper Toys.)

Part of Hasbro's success was based on its then CEO, the late Brian Goldner's, view that the company could get movies made based on its intellectual property. The logic: The main benefit was not the revenue from the movies themselves, but a boost in sales to the underlying intellectual property (the toys, the merchandise) resulting from the movies' promotion. This wound up to be true. The first movie was *Transformers*, at Paramount, directed by Michael Bay. Not only was the movie a hit, but Hasbro sold more Autobots and Decepticons.

The second film was *G.I. Joe*, also a hit, and also effective at selling more Hasbro action figures. With the success of these two movies, Hasbro management became enamored with getting deeper into the film business. And Hasbro wanted to make more movies, and sell more toys, based on some of their lesser-known intellectual property.

Just one problem: Hasbro really didn't have any access to movie distribution, which was still dominated by the major studios. And the studios didn't seem particularly interested in making movies based on the lesser intellectual property. (There's a reason you haven't seen the films *Mr. Potato Head* or *Cabbage Patch Kids 2.*)

So if the other studios weren't interested in distribution, what could Hasbro do? They began a search for another solution.

At one board session in 2014, I arrived in Providence, where Hasbro is headquartered, the day before the meeting. I was in my hotel room when I got a call from an investment banker we dealt with, both in Hasbro and outside of Hasbro, who was one of the absolute principal bankers—if not *the* principal banker—in all of media financing.

"We've been approached by Hasbro," he said over the phone. "We've been approached to help finance the acquisition of Dream-Works Animation, and we just want to make sure it's okay with the board."

Now this was an unusual question. This was the first time that I, as a board member, and I believe that *any* of the board members, had heard anything about a possible takeover of DreamWorks Animation, which was run by Jeffrey Katzenberg. Jeffrey was a genius at animated motion pictures. He's a legend and the key executive behind classics that range from *The Little Mermaid* to *The Lion King* to *Shrek*—but in 2014 he had run into a cold streak. Katzenberg had tried to pull back his personal involvement from the films still in development, and he had delegated that responsibility to the next generation of management . . . which was not going so well.

Then there was the price tag. It soon became apparent that Dream-Works sought a valuation of something on the order of $3 billion, even though it had lost money in the prior year. And it was losing money in the current year. And it was likely to keep losing money.

So on that phone call with the banker, I said, "Look, it's news to me. I think it's a terrible idea for a variety of reasons." The core reason was this: Hasbro needed feature film distribution domestically and internationally—or at least *access* to distribution—but DreamWorks didn't have that. They didn't have distribution at the time, and they were not likely to create it in the future. (Some context: DreamWorks Animation typically partnered with other studios for distribution— Paramount for many years, then 20th Century Fox, and Universal. They weren't distributors.) So if DreamWorks didn't have the main thing Hasbro was seeking, why should Hasbro spend $3 billion?

I went to the board meeting the next day. And lo and behold, Brian Goldner, the CEO, raised the prospect of acquiring Dream-Works Animation. I was the only member of the board who had any substantial experience in the motion picture business. (Hasbro was a toy company, after all.) I was very much bothered by both the governance issue—of the board not being notified—and the lack of a strategic fit. And the price sure seemed hard to justify. But Brian pitched the board, and the board seemed receptive. At the very least, they were receptive to the idea of exploring it a bit further.

Then I spoke up.

I stated my feelings, and I didn't hold back. I told the board it was a gigantic mistake to acquire DreamWorks Animation. It was expensive, it was overvalued, and it would essentially represent a bet of the entire company of Hasbro. Plus, I knew the real strength in DreamWorks Animation was Jeffrey Katzenberg himself, and Jeffrey was, in my opinion—regardless of what he might have said to Brian—really not willing to work for anyone, as he'd been an entrepreneur for almost twenty years, ever since leaving Disney in 1994.

Despite all of these arguments, there was an element on the board that felt we should defer to the CEO and take it one step further. I wasn't in a position to overrule. I clearly was not in favor of the deal, but the next step was a visit to California, to tour the DreamWorks offices in Glendale, and to see whether it made sense to keep pursuing the deal.

So the board went out to California. (It wasn't a long trip for me, as we lived in Los Angeles at this point.) We met at Jeffrey Katzenberg's home for dinner. The next day we took a tour of the DreamWorks facilities, we had a demonstration of their animation capabilities, and we talked about their future projects.

We then retired to lunch, only to discover that the *LA Times*, *Variety*, and *The Hollywood Reporter* had received, that very day, a piece written by an unnamed, anonymous member of senior management from DreamWorks Animation . . . who was dramatically opposed to the acquisition by Hasbro.

Now here's what I found interesting: The Hasbro board was taken aback by this leak from within DreamWorks' ranks. In fact, they were more focused on the leak than on the substance of the deal itself! The other board members didn't seem to think much about how, if the deal went through, there could be a very real threat to Hasbro's future.

But we never got to that point, as the board rapidly concluded that these were not people that we wanted to be in business with. So they cut the day short. We stopped the discussions. And we all got home a little earlier than we had planned.

DreamWorks Animation was later purchased by Universal Studios, and has subsequently disappeared from the landscape. Hasbro, fortunately, has gone on to bigger and better things. It's now one of the clear leaders of the toy industry worldwide. But it just goes to demonstrate, at least in my mind, that despite the prowess of a company in its field, when that company wanders too far from home, so to speak, in terms of acquisition possibilities, it runs a distinct risk of an unhappy ending. Companies need to understand what value they bring to the marketplace and build off that base; they also need to be clear about not only the valuations assigned to potential investments but also the value those investments can and cannot bring to the picture.

We got lucky with this one. And I would add that in any successful organization, from time to time, you need a fair degree of luck.

Edgar Bronfman's Quest for the Dying Record Business

JANE

It's one thing to make a mistake when assessing the value of a new product, a new employee, or a new acquisition. But what if you mis-value an entire industry? This is what happened in 1998 when my father's last billionaire boss (Edgar Bronfman Jr.) decided that the value in the future was in the record industry. Also, note that when my father shares this story, he barely mentions the expansion of *Law & Order*—condensing the importance to a single sentence and downplaying his significance. Very much on-brand.

FRANK

In early 1996, when I left Viacom, I got a call from Edgar Bronfman Jr., who was the new CEO of Seagram's, the parent company of Universal Studios.

"Look, you know I've taken control of Universal Studios, and I need a CEO," Edgar said. "And this seems to be a perfect match for you, given your background in the business."

I had to agree. But now, in hindsight, I should have kept in mind that old adage that if something seems too good to be true, it probably is.

Universal was stumbling at the time, but we could see the upside. Seagram's had already started to cut some costs and improve the overall performance, and hired some executives—some before I came on, like Ron Meyer and Greg Meidel—and then we brought in others afterward, including Ken Solomon.

The long and short of it? We were able to make some marginal improvements in the film division, and we were building the second location in Florida for the theme park, which would ultimately contribute to stronger performance for the parks division. We were creating a park in Osaka, Japan. The television division had started a turnaround, somewhat based on the expansion of Dick Wolf's *Law & Order* series, which resulted, of course, in many, many other spinoffs.

The improvements also came from a lawsuit that Edgar had the good sense (and courage) to file against Viacom. Universal and Paramount, at this point a Viacom subsidiary, were the two partners in a USA Networks Sci-Fi partnership. The partnership agreement (which I had been a part of, both when I was at Viacom and now at Universal) had a clause in it that said, essentially, *A partner cannot operate a basic cable network outside of the partnership itself.* And obviously Viacom operated around eight, nine, ten basic cable networks, which they wholly owned outside of the partnership. This seemed like a breach of the deal.

A lawsuit commenced in Delaware, which ultimately caused a trial. The judge drafted an opinion in Universal's favor, and said, basically, *You have 60 to 90 days to work this out between you, or I'm going to issue this [decision against Viacom] as a final opinion.* Viacom recognized that they had lost. So we commenced a negotiation to buy out their half of the partnership.

Which Seagram's did, for $1.8 billion, to my recollection. We purchased half, and now we had a real growth engine inside Universal, that we owned 100 percent of. We started looking around to find a new head of USA Networks, hoping to reenergize the programming.

Enter a character you've seen before: Barry Diller. This was now a few years after Diller had failed to acquire Paramount (see p. 94).

What I was *not* aware of was that Diller, who had long mentored Edgar Bronfman Jr., had gotten in touch with my billionaire boss and suggested that his (Diller's) public company could purchase the USA partnership and Universal Television, which was starting to become profitable, for $3.8 billion. But Diller added one condition to this deal: Edgar wasn't allowed to inform me.

When Edgar finally did tell me about it, he said that there was no way he would undo it. He added that we weren't really *giving up* USA Networks and Universal Television, because Universal would end up with a 45 percent equity ownership (to my memory) in Barry Diller's public company, so we would maintain a smaller, but still significant, interest in the operations of those two networks, plus Barry's nascent public company, which was renamed USA Networks.

Subsequent to the close, Edgar turned his attention away from buying up television businesses and began to push very hard to take a look at buying EMI, which was one of the four record labels that still existed. (The four record labels: Universal owned Geffen, a smaller group. Then there was Warner Music. And PolyGram, the largest. And then EMI.)

Edgar conducted lengthy negotiations with the CEO of EMI, and we were unable to reach a price that the two parties could agree on. Quickly the focus shifted to the much larger PolyGram. This was a much easier acquisition, but much more expensive . . . somewhere in the range of $12 to $14 billion. (Shades of Redstone pursuing Paramount, no matter the costs.)

As all this was happening, a new music application hit the internet: Napster. Which, of course, allowed people to easily share individual song files over the internet for the first time—and for free. There was a wide belief in the industry that Napster wouldn't be successful, because it dealt with singles, and there's no real market for singles. So even with the looming threat of Napster, Universal closed the acquisition of PolyGram at the top of the music industry market. We know what happened next—Napster proved to be a mighty disrupter of the music industry's success, as teens and adults all over the world began to accumulate and swap music tracks, as opposed to buying new ones on CDs.

This was in 1998, and it was apparent that my role at Universal was getting squeezed down, as Edgar wanted to run the music division day-to-day, and we had sold off the cable assets and the television assets, where I had most of my expertise. Then one day in November of '98, I got a call from a reporter at the *LA Times* saying, "Hey, I hear you're out at Universal."

I laughed and said, "Well, that's news to me, but it wouldn't surprise me if this is the way I find out about it."

And of course it was true. When I talked to Edgar, he confirmed that he wanted to part ways. We did, and the company continued to operate, but the EBITDA began to dramatically shrink, because of the impact of Napster and digital.

So Seagram's found itself in the position of having to sell Universal Studios, which included the music division, and then they had to *repurchase* Universal Television and the USA Networks, and Sci-Fi Networks from Diller's company at a hefty premium.

They were under a fair amount of pressure to sell. And mass media holding company Vivendi, which was then run by an entrepreneurial CEO named Jean-Marie Messier, wanted to expand in the entertainment business, and was prepared to buy *all* of Universal—including the slumping music business.

That deal closed long after I departed. Over a relatively short period of time, the Vivendi stock began to rapidly depreciate, partially due to the stress on the music business. Seagram's market capitalization had depreciated somewhere between six and nine billion dollars, thanks to the purchase of Universal, the subsequent sale of the networks and Universal Television, then the subsequent *repurchase*, along with the purchase of PolyGram music at the top of the market . . . and basically never recovered. NBC merged with Universal in 2004, and Comcast acquired NBC Universal a few years later.

The Sale of Madison Square Garden

JANE

In the 1993–94 NBA and NHL seasons, my dad went to many Knicks games at Madison Square Garden (MSG), and I joined him as often as I could (and I even went to some away ones, too). I have great memories of those games, including celebrating my birthday the night the Rangers won the Stanley Cup at home, and then being at the Knicks game during the infamous "O.J. Simpson chase," when all the networks switched coverage from basketball to the white Ford Bronco on the 405 freeway. (We didn't even know the O.J. chase was happening until halftime, when we left the court to get food and then saw the televised coverage.)

Running Viacom did have some perks, and a big one involved a company we owned for a few special years, thanks to the Paramount acquisition: Madison Square Garden.

In the early '90s, from a business perspective, Madison Square Garden was kind of limping along, only making about $30 million. But at the same time, the Knicks and the Rangers were championship-caliber teams. The Rangers won the Stanley Cup in '94, and I was even given a Rangers championship ring. (That's right: Mark Messier, Adam Graves, and Frank Biondi.)

And the Knicks came about as close as you can get to a championship. I still sometimes think of Game 6 of the 1994 NBA Finals, with the Knicks up in the series 3–2, and John Starks taking what would have been a game- (and series-) winning three-pointer . . . only to have the shot blocked by the Houston Rockets' Hakeem Olajuwon. The Rockets went on to win the game and the championship. But such is sports.

We had some coveted seats at the Garden, and were lucky to see all of this action in person. When Viacom owned MSG, the company was allotted eight courtside tickets to each Knicks game. They were across from the scorer's table, not far from Spike Lee. Four of these seats were reserved for friends of the Garden, celebrities, and that kind of thing. And four were for the ownership, and I had discretion over who used those four tickets.

My daughter Jane was a giant sports fan and went to almost every home game in the second half of the '93–'94 Knicks season, after we became owners of the Garden and the two teams. But the shareholders always come first, and we decided to sell the Garden, in 1995, to a partnership of Cablevision and the ITT Corporation, for $1.1 billion. This helped us pay down Viacom's heavy debt, largely incurred from the $9.7 billion Paramount acquisition. It was a good deal for us. As *The New York Times* said, "Many analysts said the purchase price of $1.075 billion in cash would far exceed the Garden's actual worth," and then, more bluntly, "The only clear victor is Viacom and its chairman, Sumner M. Redstone, because financial analysts had generally placed the Garden's value at $600 million to $800 million."

We knew the deal made sense, but we sure would miss those seats. Then someone special had an interesting idea. Before the deal was finalized, one day Jane—still in high school—asked me, "Can you keep the tickets?" I just laughed. She explained she didn't mean that me, personally, would keep the tickets, but rather . . . could Viacom?

So I sent in the request. As luck would have it, somehow the lawyers hammering out the negotiations did not address the request until the eleventh hour of papering the deal, literally in the middle of the night. The general counsel called me, as they were in the final stages of negotiations, preparing to sign the contracts.

Our general counsel asked, "Are you [Viacom] willing to pay for them?"

Now I didn't have the guts to say anything other than, "Yes, of course we'll pay for them."

We couldn't have asked for these seats free of charge until the end of time; that would have been a ridiculous request that nobody would have agreed to. But retaining these seats—at the fair prices we were paying—would be a coup. The issue was less about the money and more about the prime location of these seats. "They didn't appreciate how good the seats were when we passed along your question," our general counsel told me over the phone in the middle of the night. "Would you be willing to accept seats in another location?"

That was an interesting question. On the one hand, we would have happily taken other seats that were just as good. Yet I knew that such seats didn't exist. So we said that, yes, we'd be willing to accept comparable seats, but then gave some strict parameters that would be awfully tough to match: the same side of the court as the current seats, mid center-court, between foul lines, and so on.

As our general counsel relayed to me, the reps at MSG said to him, "Great, thanks, we really appreciate your willingness to work with us."

And because this was literally in the middle of the night, the buyers—Cablevision and ITT—didn't do any more due diligence, and they papered the deal. We now had these seats in the official contract because we understood the value of what we were asking and the buyers did not.

This meant that MSG's new owners had a problem on their hands: They contractually owed us these seats, but there were no other available seats that met the requirements.

Their solution? Create new seats.

To creatively honor the contract, the Garden added new courtside seats by filling in the aisles where they reached the court, effectively creating new inventory. It changed the seating plan. More specifically, the Knicks altered how they configured the front row around the entire court, and this change led to roughly twenty additional courtside seats.

Other NBA teams took notice. *You can add extra seats to the front row?* More seats meant more revenue. And the NBA is a copycat league, so soon other major-market teams began to follow the Knicks' lead, adding more seats in the same fashion. I don't know if every NBA franchise followed suit, but I know the Celtics did, the Bulls did, the Lakers did, and so on. All the major market teams did it.

The move created twenty extra seats, and each seat—at that point—went for around $3,500 per game. Every season you have forty-one home games, plus preseason and possible playoffs, so let's call it fifty games per year, roughly. The math works out to around $3.5 million of incremental revenue for one team, and for one year.

JANE

Viacom's seats were as good as they get. We often saw Spike Lee just a few feet away, and then the occasional celebrity power couple like Tom Cruise and Nicole Kidman, or Richard Gere and Cindy Crawford. One night I sat right next to Richard Gere, who told me that he hadn't been to a basketball game since before the three-point line was added in 1979. About six months later, Gere and Crawford announced their divorce. When *US Weekly* and *People* showed a picture of the couple in the news stories, there I was seated next to Richard Gere. Before social media and 24/7 paparazzi, the press relied on pictures from public appearances, and that must have been one of their last joint public outings. Dad loved telling this story about what he called "Jane's seats."

Sumner Redstone Could Have Been (Really, Really) Rich

JANE

When it comes to "value analysis," this is maybe the ultimate *What If* . . . What if Sumner had never tried to acquire Paramount? My father does the math and plays it out.

FRANK

Sumner Redstone was rich. That cannot be denied. But he could have been Bill Gates– or even Warren Buffett–level rich.

When National Amusements—Sumner's family's movie theater company—acquired Viacom in 1987, the result was a highly lever-aged company with vastly underoptimized assets, particularly with the MTV Networks. Shortly thereafter, I was brought on board to run Viacom, and set on a course to slash the debt (by selling some of our cable assets). Then MTV and Nickelodeon took off, unlocking revenue and profit growth; they sold ads for the first time in their history and built quite a successful audience.

As I talked about in a previous chapter, Viacom went on to acquire Paramount in 1994, which diluted the stock. After I left Viacom, the shareholder base was even further diluted in 1999 by the merger with CBS.

Years later, I began to wonder what would have happened if these deals never took place. How would it have impacted Sumner's wealth?

Looking at it in retrospect, and recognizing that hindsight is perfect, Sumner and National Amusements owned 92 percent of Viacom when they acquired it in 1987.

What happened between 1987 and 1994 was that the EBITDA for the MTV Networks alone approached $2–$2.5 billion. At its high, this would have been valued around *$50 billion* as an enterprise unto itself.

At that time, Viacom also had a million cable subscribers that were worth about $3 billion. We had a broadcast TV and radio group that was worth about a billion and change. And we had a TV production company that distributed *The Cosby Show*, which was also worth about a billion dollars.

When you do all the arithmetic? The valuation for the company would have been in the mid-$50 billions, or nearly $60 billion. And Sumner owned 92 percent. So, rough justice, that would have put his net worth between $45 billion and $50 billion in the early '90s . . . putting him on par with Warren Buffett and Bill Gates. (And well ahead of his other unofficial rival, Rupert Murdoch.)

JANE

At the time of his death in 2020, *Forbes* estimated Sumner's net worth at $2.6 billion. Still an extremely wealthy man, but catching his white whale of the movie business came at a staggering price, perhaps in part because he never really understood what things were worth.

The King Brothers

JANE

Here is another example of people who, with Dad's guidance, acted on what they valued . . . and became very, very rich.

FRANK

Shortly after I left Universal Studios in 1998, I received a call from Michael King. He's one of the King Brothers who controlled King World, and they were the distributors of *Wheel of Fortune*, *Jeopardy!*, the *Oprah Winfrey Show*, and a few others. I had gotten to know them well, and they had done a fine job with those two shows for Merv Griffin and then for Coca-Cola.

I had maintained a good relationship with them during my tenure at Viacom, including an almost-acquisition of King World by Viacom, which fell apart after a handshake.

Michael called to say that, unlike in past years, they had decided that they were no longer content with just being successful distributors. They wanted to expand their universe. And they'd like to talk to me about working with them to acquire other media enterprises.

I went to Michael's house to meet with him and his advisors and his brothers. It became apparent that far from being in acquisition mode, they relayed that they had two offers to be purchased: one by CBS and one by Fox Family, which was co-owned by Fox and Haim Saban, the entrepreneur.

They wanted help in considering the two options, which were clearly both attractive, but very different in terms of risk and reward. This presented an interesting dilemma.

"It really boils down to your risk preference," I explained to them. Fox Family was a single, successful cable network, and, on paper, it looked like the company would continue to be extremely successful, would probably grow, and its value would climb quite rapidly. On the other hand, CBS would be a slow and steady grower with a nice dividend payout.

We decided to take meetings with both parties.

As it happened, although we accurately analyzed the risk preferences, it became apparent that the Fox Family really wanted only one of the King Brothers, and had no desire to keep the other brothers on.

This was deeply offensive to the King family, and I think it heavily influenced their decision; regardless of the merits of the Fox Family offer, they were inclined to take the CBS offer. Which they did, and it resulted in a handsome premium for all the King World shareholders.

As a bonus, about a month and a half after they signed the CBS deal, it was announced that Viacom was going to take over CBS in an all-stock deal . . . that was well above the price that the Kings had negotiated with CBS.

So, in effect, they sold King World productions twice in a period of ninety days. And were handsomely rewarded for doing so.

Law & Order & the Birth of TV Franchises (by Ken Solomon)

JANE

My father took the reins at Universal Studios in 1996. This also put him in charge of Universal Television, which, at the time, produced a little show called *Law & Order*. It had not yet become a cultural phenomenon. It wasn't even clear if it would be renewed. My father had hired Ken Solomon to run Universal's domestic TV department, and he told me a story about how my father clearly saw the value in creative ideas—and how, away from the headlines, Dad empowered his team to deliver content to viewers in surprising ways. We now take the idea of TV spin-offs and franchises for granted, but in some ways, it started with *Law & Order*. I'll let Ken take it from here.

KEN

When I got to Universal, *Law & Order* had been on the air for around six years. It hadn't yet won any Emmys or critical acclaim. It was a solid show with a loyal fan base, but it was probably going to go off the air, because the costs were getting higher each season—for the actors, the directors, the producers. It was questionable whether we'd renew it. I said to Frank, "Look, I think this is worth saving, but it's going to take resources." He agreed, so we doubled down and renewed all the writers and the actors. Then the show started taking off. We won the Emmy. Dick Wolf (creator of *Law & Order*) was telling me we had zero chance of winning the Emmy, but we did.

That's when we came up with the idea of a true full-on sequel to *Law & Order*. (Credit for the original idea, of course, goes to Dick Wolf.) It was originally titled *Sex Crimes*, although that name wouldn't necessarily be great for the advertisers. And when *Law & Order* was up for renewal at NBC, we came up with a strategy for selling them **both** *Law & Order* and what was then called *Sex Crimes*. We bundled the two shows. This strategy had some risk. What if NBC wanted *Law & Order* but nothing to do with *Sex Crimes*? And we proposed something that had never been done before. *Sex Crimes* would air after *Law & Order* on NBC, and then *Sex Crimes* would run again on USA (which we at Universal owned) during the same week that both shows ran on NBC, so NBC might be afraid it would cut into their own ratings. Again, there was real risk. A lot of CEOs wouldn't take this chance. We already had a good thing with *Law & Order*, and this attempt to build a franchise might backfire.

But Frank saw the value and he backed the play. And a couple of things happened. *Sex Crimes*, of course, became *Law & Order: Special Victims Unit*. And it turned *Law & Order* from a TV show into an endless franchise. Now we had two shows on NBC and another on our own cable channel (USA). That was *heretical* at the time. People thought the network would never go for it. But they did. Frank innately understood the value of this, and now the value to Universal of this franchise is almost incalculable. He got it. He knew it.

This play/release pattern became the industry standard when selling big, expensive dramas to networks as the shows got bigger and costs for these series skyrocketed. It became expected (and a badge of honor) for a show to have a second play on basic cable (including hits like all three of Jerry Bruckheimer's CSI series), and it all started with Frank's green light of *Law & Order: SVU* for both networks.

Balancing Value and Values

My father also knew how to prioritize personal values, had unfailing judgment, and he was always my most trusted source of wisdom. He was always in my corner, always willing to share his perspective and advice—careful to qualify it as his own, so that I would not mistake it for his expectations of me.

For example, when I finally managed to land a full-time job in baseball—marketing with the Los Angeles Dodgers—my first few seasons were a childhood dream brought to life. I learned a ton. But it eventually became clear that this would not always be the case; I had six different bosses in the first two years. When the seventh arrived I was exhausted, frustrated, and less enchanted with working in professional baseball.

So I talked to my father about this tough career choice, weighing the pros and cons of leaving. He emailed me some advice that was so practical, so sound, and so thoughtful that I refer to it to this day.

I'm sure he never intended this email to be published in a book, but it gives a good sense of how he thoughtfully analyzed the nuance, considered both sides, and ultimately how he measured and evaluated both value and values. Here's the full email from Dad, with a few annotations from me:

> As kids we really got no exposure to finances and had only a small weekly allowance. My folks paid for the big stuff, but everything else we had to earn. As a result, in college, I rarely had more than $5 in my pocket. I did very little that required spending any money. It was not always "fun."
>
> When I got out of business school, I had no idea what I wanted to do, largely because I had never been exposed to business until I was in business school. I also wanted to make money so that I could be secure and independent. I went into investment banking because I was good with numbers

and the pay was tops if you succeeded. I did that instead of going into the media business (which I thought might be fun) because I enjoyed watching it so much, and it seemed wrong to be doing something "frivolous" even if I could find the right entry level job.

Note that Dad didn't use the word "sizzle" here, but it was clear to me that he was thinking about the merits of substance. He continues:

> I stayed with banking from 1968 until 1972 in 3 different jobs. I was pretty good at it, but I hated the fact that you could not specialize in one industry (never felt I was developing expertise in a field) and I hated the customer solicitation part of the job (I still hate the phone). So I quit and started consulting independently with some old colleagues to pay the bills. This ultimately led to TelePrompTer which is where I met your mother and got into the cable industry.
>
> Even that had a lot of twists and turns . . . but most of those early jobs were disappointing and boring. It was very serendipitous that I wound up at HBO where I had my first real success at 34 years old.
>
> Looking back, **going entirely for money was not totally fulfilling, but it gave me the freedom to live nicely and try a number of things until I found something that "worked" for me**.

I added the bold; Dad didn't include that in the email, but this is an important concept. Sometimes we dismiss the role of compensation in our analysis, thinking it's almost crass to be motivated by money. Yet compensation can provide you options, and if you're not sure what you want to do, it can help you bide time until something clicks.

What is interesting is what constituted "working." [At HBO] it was not so much the type of job, pay television, but that we had a business that was growing, a "team" that in many respects was dysfunctional and competitive with each other, but was kicking butt in the marketplace. Winning tends to be fun. The winning spawned credit to all, and most of us went on to new and better roles because we had created a name and economic value. Work was fun because we were winning! It was not because it was TV.

Now how does this apply to you? First, we are different people . . . I don't sense you feel the same need to make a sizable net worth, which is fine. So your decisions are driven more by your likes—something I never felt I had the freedom to do.

Second, I am far from convinced that pursuing (and even capturing) a dream will provide job satisfaction. It has a lot more to do with whom you are doing it, and how successful the enterprise is in the market.

This cuts against the grain of the usual "follow your dreams!" platitudes, but it's also advice that's rooted in reality.

Third, there is the "skill set" issue. I could always add and subtract, but I also had a small gift of seeing things in those trends and numbers that others did not. For a long time it was hard to sell that on a resume, since organizations are not looking for solvers of yet-to-be-defined problems except at the CEO level. Working in an emerging industry was really the key to me using those skills for their best result.

Buried in here is another nugget of wisdom: To showcase skills that might go unnoticed in a larger or more established company, it can be helpful to cut your teeth in an emerging industry. For my father that meant TelePrompTer and the early days of cable; for today's professionals that could be the world of start-ups.

I think you have great people skills. You are organized and disciplined and you have endless energy with a great work ethic. In theory, you could pick your domain—finance, marketing, sales, general management.

I think you should seek out a position that will pay you . . . Pay is a scorecard that validates worth and effort and provides a measuring stick versus your peers.

Here I'm reminded of the earlier chapters of Dad's career, during his TelePrompTer and Topper Toys days, where he hadn't yet truly found his groove. He later found his way into the media space, but his guiding words were to not put too much stock in a particular job. He appreciated that I had pursued a path (baseball) that I thought would be interesting, but thought there was no need to stick to it as a matter of principle. A job, after all, is just a job. Paychecks matter.

CHAPTER 9

Embrace Luck (Good and Bad)

JANE

Sometimes the role of luck can be obvious, like when a traffic jam causes you to miss a flight. But luck can have a more subtle impact. It's easy to overlook the sneaky role that serendipity can play in our lives, and this is something that my father learned early on.

"My first encounter with serendipity was in my senior year in high school," he told me in the very first story that he shared for this book. If not for the good luck of having some surprising connections at Princeton, my father explains, his career might have taken a very different path. He never lost sight of this serendipity, which helped keep him grounded throughout his career.

It's important to make your own luck, yes, but you can also have the humility and emotional intelligence to acknowledge where you benefit from forces beyond your control. This is a concept that Malcolm Gladwell explores in *Outliers*. "People don't rise from nothing. We do owe something to parentage and patronage," Gladwell writes. "The people who stand before kings may look like they did it all by themselves. But in fact they are invariably the beneficiaries of hidden advantages and extraordinary opportunities and cultural legacies that allow them to learn and work hard and make sense of the world in ways others cannot."

What do Bill Gates, Paul Allen, Steve Ballmer, Eric Schmidt, and Steve Jobs have in common? Yes, they were all Silicon Valley titans, but as Gladwell explains, they all have a sneakier connection: they were all born around the same time . . . in the perfect time and place to capitalize on the looming silicon boom. Bill Gates: born in 1955. Paul Allen: 1953. Steve Ballmer: 1956. Eric Schmidt: 1955. And Steve Jobs: 1955.

Why does this matter? Bill Gates went to a high school in 1968 that gave him access to a mainframe computer terminal, a rare opportunity denied to 99.9 percent of other Americans, granting him a massive head start on learning to code. That's not to take anything away from Bill Gates. He was smart and hungry and he made the absolute most of his opportunity . . . but he couldn't have done it without that timing and some luck. And crucially, if he were *older*, then he would have already had a mid-career job and wouldn't have had the same opportunity or time to learn how to code. If he were *younger*, it might have been too late. Gates and these others were lucky enough to be born in the perfect time.

Just as these tech icons were in the right place at the right time in Silicon Valley, my father just happened to enter the cable industry—and in particular pay TV—as it launched its multi-decade bull run. This was part luck, part savvy. Dad suspected the cable industry had a bright future, which is one reason he chose to work at TelePrompTer instead of a different field. He even had a phrase for this kind of mindset: "Swim with the tide." And he liked to joke (with typical self-deprecation), "If you were in the cable industry from the '70s to the '90s, you'd have to be really incompetent not to be successful."

Of course, getting blessed with good fortune is only part of the equation. You need to make the most of it. After all, in 1968, there were other high school students living near Bill Gates who had the same access that he did; almost none of them took advantage. Luck isn't enough without doing the work, mastering the details, partnering for the long term, and embracing the rest of my father's principles.

And there's an art to knowing the difference between skill and luck. When you're dealt four aces in poker, do you win that hand because of skill? (And if you think this sounds like a too obvious example, consider Dad's story "I Don't Believe in Luck," later in this chapter). Sometimes when you're in an intense negotiation, you can catch a lucky break, get more than you bargained for, and then your job is to simply keep a straight face and count your good fortune (as you'll see in the stories about the James Bond and Rambo negotiations). Sometimes you think you're about to move across the country—and you've already found a new home and put your kids in a new school, and they're even throwing you a goodbye party just as you leave—and then, out of nowhere, you get a job offer you absolutely cannot refuse (such as running Viacom), and that stroke of luck changes everything.

Leverage Is a Strange Beast

JANE

This is a quick throwback to earlier in my father's career, at HBO, when he was still negotiating with the film studios. And as he learned here, sometimes negotiations simply come down to getting lucky.

FRANK

When I was head of HBO in the early '80s, we acquired content by negotiating with basically every motion picture studio. At the time, MGM-UA was a perennial "runner-up" in the box office sweepstakes, but one year, in 1982, they had two very successful films: *First Blood* (the original Rambo) and a James Bond film. And then they also had a bunch of pictures that have never been heard of since—some real turkeys, including *Inchon*, the epic Korean War pic starring Laurence Olivier, which had a budget of $46 million and drew in a box office of $5.2 million and currently has a Rotten Tomatoes score of 0 percent. (They never made an *Inchon 2*.)

We were negotiating how much to pay MGM for the right to license their content on HBO. This year was a real battle. We offered very little money for the seven or eight turkeys that they bundled with Rambo and James Bond, they balked, and we were at something of an impasse. (Typically, you bought all of the pictures from every studio—the good and the bad.)

About a week into our deadlock, we got a call from one of their senior negotiators who said, "We'd like to make a counterproposal."

Okay. We were open to new ideas. We assumed that they would offer another price for the bundle, but instead they came back and said, "We will sell you Bond and Rambo for three million apiece, and we'll put a pin in the rest of the conversation."

For perspective, $3 million was basically fair-market value for those pictures. That was a reasonable rate. And this meant that we *wouldn't* need to also buy the turkeys. *Why would they offer this?*

Now, there may have been some earnings pressures within MGM-UA that forced their hand. But regardless of the reason, this gave us tremendous leverage in the future, as it let us bid *whatever we wanted* on the turkeys. This had never before happened with any other studio. The offer was so appealing, you have to kind of control your voice and say, "Let me think about that and get back to you" when what you're really thinking is, "YES, WE'LL TAKE IT!"

Sometimes life surprises you, even in negotiations where the leverage is unclear.

"I Don't Believe in Luck"

JANE

My father chose to embrace luck, and to have the humility to appreciate its role. Others took the opposite approach.

FRANK

In the early 1990s at Viacom, we were on a "road show" to raise equity for the company. On the way back from Europe, on a private jet, we started a card game between the senior management team, Redstone, and myself.

We played a game called Night Baseball, which is a notorious wildcard game—it's not uncommon to have a full house, four-of-a-kind, or even a five-of-a-kind.

Midway through the game, I looked at my hand: Five kings. The betting got heavier and heavier, and a mountain of chips began to form on the table. More betting, more chips. Finally it came to a call.

Our CFO had five tens. Our investment banker had five jacks.

Another had five queens. I had five kings, and I felt pretty good about it, and then Redstone looked at us with a smile on his face.

"Read 'em and weep, five aces," Redstone said.

Everybody groaned, and sort of collectively said, *Oh, come on.*

"I thought I played that brilliantly," said Redstone, pleased with himself.

"Excuse me?" I said. "What was so brilliant about the way you played that?"

"Well," Redstone said, a little surprised, "I kept you guys all in."

"Sumner, you couldn't have gotten me out with a gun," I said. "Five kings, are you kidding me? What are the odds you're going to have five aces?" The truth was that he just got lucky.

"I don't believe in luck," Redstone said.

Maybe so, but boy did he have a lot of it.

Tom Cruise Money

In one small way I even helped in a lucky break of my father's career. When I was at Princeton, I became good friends with a woman who would go on to date noted financier Carl Icahn's son. She vacationed with him and his family one summer on a yacht, and stopped by to visit our summer home. Although my father and Carl knew of each other, that was the first time they met in person, and they stayed in touch.

So in 2006, when Carl Icahn waged a proxy fight against Time Warner, guess who he tapped to propose as the company's new CEO?

This resulted in a lucky opportunity. After decades of hard work and exactly the right experience and understanding of the company he once had a hand in leading, Carl offered him a lucrative job that ended up requiring just a few days of work.

In the early 2000s, Time Warner was still recovering from its merger with AOL, and its stock price had suffered. Carl Icahn announced that he had accumulated an ownership position in Time Warner, and retained leading investment firm Lazard Freres to do an analysis of how much the company's individual pieces should be valued. Carl believed they were worth more than the market was currently valuing the whole company. He would then wage a proxy fight if Time Warner did not agree to his demands to sell off different pieces of the company, to maximize value.

I received a phone call from Bruce Wasserstein and my late brother, Mike Biondi, who were, respectively, the CEO and co-head of investment banking at Lazard.

They said, "You know, Carl is bound and determined to follow through with Time Warner, and he needs to put together a slate of board of directors nominees, as well as a nominee for chairman of the board. He's prepared to pay you $6 million—in success or failure—if you'd be willing to run as a nominee of chairman of the board."

Now, I had been a long-term personal shareholder of Time Warner, and I'd been somewhat disappointed in its performance, so I was sympathetic to Carl's position. Before I answered, I asked Bruce and my brother if they could send me their analysis—their quite extensive analysis—of the Time Warner valuation.

I read it. It was several hundred pages long, and it was thoughtfully done. And it basically indicated that if the pieces of Time Warner were sold off individually—cable, the studio, Home Box Office, its interest in AOL—the proceeds, on a pretax basis, would be substantially higher than the current stock price of Time Warner.

So I got back to my brother and said, "I'd be happy to do it. What would it entail?" They said they had a presentation scheduled in about three days in New York, and if I could get to New York to participate, that would be great. Which I did.

The primary part of the presentation was done by Lazard, then Carl and I spoke for a bit, then we did a Q&A. After it was over, I think the feeling was that we made a successful case for the evaluation. We then spoke to individual shareholders on a one-on-one basis. It became apparent that there was a good deal of sympathy for Carl's analysis, and the inherent discrepancy between the current share price and the value of the sum of the parts.

What *wasn't* apparent—but began to become so—was that virtually none of the shareholders were prepared to vote out an entire board of directors. So after two days of these presentations, and getting these consistent results, Carl decided to call off his proxy fight. He could deal just based on the merits of the analysis. Which he did, and he ultimately made a fair amount of money, as did some of his proxy fight partners.

I flew back to California after what was, basically, three or four days' worth of (very lucrative) work. Carl called to say thanks. He added, jokingly, "You were making more on an hourly basis than Tom Cruise."

I laughed. "Quite honestly, Carl, for a short period of time, I think I was making more than you were on an hourly basis."

I thanked him, and that was the end of a rather short and interesting adventure in proxy fights.

A Picture's Worth a Thousand Deals

In the summer of 1985, after Coca-Cola had closed on the purchase of Embassy, we were in the process of closing down Embassy Films, which had been fairly unprofitable, and also selling Embassy Home Video. One willing buyer was Andre Blay, who, justifiably, had been known as the Father of the Home Video Industry, because he had successfully convinced 20th Century Fox to sell him all of their future home video rights in the early '80s . . . and when they realized what a colossal mistake they made, they repurchased it for $100-plus million.

I wasn't personally handling the deal. It kept going back and forth, with our people at Coca-Cola insisting that Andre's offer was wildly, ridiculously low, and Andre's people insisting that we were ignoring a bona fide offer. I finally got a call from Alan Schwartz, who was then head of Bear Stearns Investment banking, and later the firm's CEO. At the time I hadn't met Alan.

Alan called and said, "Look, I'm representing Andre, and he feels like he's getting bum treatment from your people. Is there any way we can have a face-to-face?"

I was more than happy to have a face-to-face, because Andre was clearly presenting to his bankers (including Alan) a deal that was much different than he presented to Coca-Cola. So we agreed to meet. We could only find a Saturday midday, so the offices were relatively empty. We met in the main conference room. After going back and forth on the deal, I think it became apparent to Alan that he wasn't getting the full story from his client.

"Could we take a time out, and just you and me go to your office and chat about this?" Alan asked.

I said sure, happily.

So we went to my office, and I sat behind my desk, and Alan sat across, facing me. We talked about the differences between the deal described in the conference room and then the deal described by Andre Blay.

For some reason, Alan kept staring over my shoulder.

Finally he said, "Excuse me. I've got to stop this for a second."

Again he looked over my shoulder, then continued, "Why do you have a picture of my daughter on your desk?"

Huh? I had no idea what he was talking about.

So I turned around and looked at the picture he was staring at. It was a picture of my oldest daughter, Anne, who was posed in the traditional Camp Mohawk annual photo.

Camp Mohawk is a day camp in Westchester, and by coincidence, Alan lived in Westchester. In the photo, Anne wore a Camp Mohawk T-shirt and stood behind a tree that had a V-shaped trunk, leaning through the V.

I looked at Alan and said, "That's not your daughter. That's my daughter."

"What?"

He went around my desk and looked at the photo more closely. "Oh my God," he said. "The resemblance is remarkable." It turned out that our daughters, coincidentally, were both around the same age, both blonde, and both gap-toothed. And they were both campers at Camp Mohawk. As Alan remembered years later, when he saw the photo of what he assumed to be his daughter, he thought, *Is this one of those shows where you show up, and somehow it turns out that this guy has taken over your life?*

And in the years that followed, Alan went on to become a longtime investment banking advisor and a good friend.

Timing Is Everything: The WaterView Investment Fund

JANE

Part of "embracing luck" is to expect that life will toss you surprises, both good and bad. In the early 2000s, my father co-founded an investment fund that focused on new media start-ups called Water-View. Many of the companies they invested in were prescient in terms of the future of digital content (allowing viewers to directly stream movies and TV shows, foreshadowing Netflix), and most of them were, ultimately, too far ahead of their time . . . and then ran into the unlucky buzzsaw of the dot-com crash. He didn't complain or gripe about this; he knew that luck can giveth, luck can taketh away. This is another story that my father didn't get the chance to share before he passed, so I've done my best to pinch-hit and fill in the blanks.

This story begins over fifty years ago. Back in 1968, after my father graduated from Harvard Business School, he began his career at the investment banking firm of Cogan, Berlind, Weill & Levitt.

One of his early coworkers was a lawyer named Rick Reiss, who quickly became a good friend. Rick was new to finance and trying to learn the ropes. "I didn't know anything about business," Rick remembers now. "I turned to Frank to ask for his help. I would ask him questions, and he would pull out his textbooks." They played softball together.

The two stayed in touch for years. Even after my father moved on to TelePrompTer and later HBO and Coca-Cola, and as Rick embarked on a successful money management career, the two remained good friends. Their softball games evolved into tennis matches. ("I would consistently lose to him every time we played tennis," Rick remembers.)

This is, of course, yet another example of partnering for the long term. Rick's family became close with our family, and as a kid, I remember visiting their house in Sagaponack, Long Island, and then in East Hampton. In one visit, their refrigerator's drinking water dispenser got jammed and would not stop running. Dad's quick thinking saved the day. He shut off the water in the basement—he was always handy—and for years Rick joked that without my father's timely plumbing help, the home would have flooded.

In the 1980s, Rick even had a cameo in one of my father's most consequential career moves. Rick happened to be acquaintances with Sumner Redstone; as an investment manager, he knew many of the industry's key players. Just after Redstone acquired Viacom, as Rick remembers it, "I was giving a presentation, and Sumner Redstone pulled me over—he knew I was very good friends with Frank—and said, 'I'm going to figure out a way to hire him.'"

Flash forward another decade. In 1999, after being ousted from Universal in a very public way, Dad had had enough of the personal whims of billionaire owners. He wanted to take a turn as his own boss. So he started an investment firm with his old friend, Rick Reiss. They called it WaterView.

The idea was to marry up Dad's industry knowledge—and endless network of connections—with Rick's investment prowess, and focus on start-ups in new media. Many of their investments were prescient. The concepts neatly tracked with how the internet would evolve today and where it's headed tomorrow: direct content to consumers, streaming services, influencers speaking directly to end users.

"These days he's putting his fingerprints on all sorts of Net-related entertainment deals, investing in a diverse group of startups with the partners at his current outfit, WaterView Advisors," John Geirland wrote in the April 2000 issue of *Wired*. "Biondi sits on the boards of eight companies that stream short and long films over the Web, aggregate broadband webcasts, hawk Pokémon figures and other licensed merchandise, and hatch big plans to serve the business-to-business needs of the global media community."

Dating back to his days at TelePrompTer, my father clearly saw the macro trends at play. "Biondi's vision of the Internet is as sober as a Monday-morning staff meeting," *Wired* continued. "The term 'interactive' seldom pops up. Biondi sees the Net as the latest development—albeit a radical one—in a 20-year trend in media that he sums up with the phrase 'What I wanna see when I wanna see it.'"

And once again, personal connections helped fuel the growth. "Hollywood is all about personal relationships, he asserts. Directors, producers, and writers will be a lot more comfortable talking to people they've worked with than to a venture capitalist," Geirland writes in the *Wired* piece. "'We get most of our really good sources of deals from friends,' Biondi maintains. 'These are people you've dealt with over the years. You can shake hands with them and you've got a deal.'"

WaterView's investments included companies like AtomFilms (distributing movies straight to customers and cutting out the middleman, à la Netflix or Amazon Prime), Broadband Sports (where athletes would create content delivered straight to fans), and Sightsound (which also delivered movies over the internet).

These ideas all look very much at home in the 2020s. Their vision was accurate. Just one tiny problem: the dot-com crash.

Thanks largely to the brutal timing of that crash, many of the WaterView investments failed. "The timing was horrendous," says Rick. "Many of the concepts worked, but it was the wrong time."

Yet one investment that he was most proud of is now a lasting legacy: The Tennis Channel.

Creation of The Tennis Channel

As you can probably tell from previous stories in this book, my father loved tennis. He loved to watch it, he loved to play it. He played with colleagues, friends, family, and even folks like Merv Griffin and Dr. Phil. He also played against a future president—more on that in a bit.

Dad was good. "Frank would be considered a top club tennis player," says Martin Shafer, who's not just the CEO of Castle Rock, but was also one of Dad's frequent tennis partners. Martin adds that unlike the many executives who use tennis as a pretext for hobnobbing, my father really cared about the game and the competition. "It wasn't a business thing for him," Martin says. "It was strictly tennis for tennis' sake. A lot of people use tennis as a way to further their business ties, but he just played with who he liked playing with."

He seemed to play everywhere. He played at John Gardiner's Tennis Ranch, in Scottsdale, Arizona. He played at the Columbia University tennis bubble in the icy Manhattan winters. He played in club tournaments most summers, where he was a seven-time singles champion, ten-time doubles champion (six in a row), and, my favorite, two-time mixed doubles champion—with me. We also lost in the finals five times.

Dad thought of tennis as a metaphor for both business and life, as it's a mix of skill, talent, grit, hard work, composure, strategy, mental fortitude, doing the right thing (no one likes to play with a cheat), and the occasional lucky bounce. He once told *The New Yorker*'s Ken Auletta, "If you watch me play tennis, I play a very good defensive game. It plays to my strengths. I'm good at analyzing a situation. I'm less confident taking the initiative. When I'm aggressive, it's because I'm very confident of the reasons and the facts on our side of the table."

How often did he play? After he passed, while looking up contact information or other information to settle his affairs, I ran across some of Dad's old emails. I was amazed by the sheer volume of messages devoted to setting up matches—*"Hey, can you play on Sunday at 2pm?"* or *"Frank, do you have a fourth for Sunday doubles?"*

So in 2001, perhaps it's no surprise that my father helped launch The Tennis Channel, as WaterView—and Dad personally—were initial investors. "About twenty years ago, a handful of visionaries got together with an audacious idea," recounts The Tennis Channel's Brett Haber, on-air during the 2020 Australian Open. "All of these people had a passion for tennis, and they were all leaders in the television industry."

This group was led by my father, who tapped Ken Solomon to run the fledgling channel.

Ken had worked for my father when he ran Universal Studios— Dad had put him in charge of Universal Television. As my father once said, Ken helped "take Universal Television from a $30 million loss in '96 to $100 million profit in '98." (That turnaround was made possible by the *Law & Order* franchise, as discussed in chapter 8.)

My father and Ken had stayed in touch, just as Dad always tended to stay in touch—more partnering for the long term. As Ken later remembered, "He called me up and said, 'I've got your next thing for you' . . . I'll never forget the call. You just remember those moments. He said, 'Well, it's The Tennis Channel,' and I just started laughing and said, 'You've got to be crazy! That's the dumbest idea. That will never work.'" Ken says that before he agreed, "I had one condition for saying yes. That Frank would be chairman of the board." But when Ken told my father that condition, he says that Dad responded, "No, I actually think *you* should be chairman."

Ken Solomon might have been skeptical, but the idea worked. As luck would have it, even though WaterView focused on new-media start-ups, it was their investment in old media—a cable channel!—that now has a twenty-year legacy. "He felt that content was so important, and The Tennis Channel would figure out ways to get distribution," says Rick Reiss, one of his WaterView partners, once again underscoring how my father's push for content-to-consumers was consistent across the decades.

Rick adds that the early days weren't easy, as my father "had to fight every day for every small little cable system that would finally agree to carry it." Those fights would spill into the courtroom, as their biggest distributor, Comcast, later refused to broadcast it to their basic cable subscribers (to avoid competing with The Golf Channel and NBC Sports Network, which they owned). Despite this, he remained close friends with Comcast's CEO, Brian Roberts, during the bitterest days of the lawsuit. While The Tennis Channel won a key decision, ultimately Comcast prevailed, limiting The Tennis Channel's subscriber base and its valuation. Even with that setback, The Tennis Channel was later acquired by Sinclair Broadcasting, and as Ken Solomon recently said, it is "at the very least a billion-dollar asset—significantly more—and has transformed the way tennis is viewed in this country."

Soon after my father passed away, during primetime coverage of the Australian Open, The Tennis Channel aired a tribute to him. "Frank was the leader. He was the center of it. When Frank did something, you knew it was going to happen, and he knew a little bit about tennis, too," said Ken in the tribute, announcing that they would dedicate the 2020 Australian Open to my father. "Frank is the reason we're here," said Ken. "There really would be no Tennis Channel without Frank Biondi."

Lucky Shots & Presidential Tennis

JANE

To end this chapter, I thought it would be appropriate to have Dad telling one of his all-time favorite tennis stories, which also involves a great deal of luck.

FRANK

I've played tennis for most of my life. In 1999, I played in a charity tennis tournament for the Prostate Cancer Foundation, then called CapCure. It was co-hosted by a certain real-estate developer. The developer was known, at the time, for being something of a liberal Democrat from New York: Donald J. Trump.

Even long before the White House, Trump had a bit of a reputation in the business world. Other CEOs knew him as a self-promoter, a guy who lobbied *Forbes* to boost the estimate of his net worth, and a guy who had some trouble paying his debts. We knew that banks had grown wary of dealing with him. I didn't personally know the guy.

Yet I'll give Trump this: he knew how to host a tennis tournament. The event was an odd mix of professional tennis players and CEOs. You'd see tennis legends like Tracy Austin sharing a court with older billionaires like Larry Tisch and Michael Milken, who was Trump's co-host. I knew Mike from my Viacom days, and he knew I had a decent tennis game, so he had said, "Look, if you'll do it, I'll give you a ride on my plane to and from." (How do you say no to that?)

So Mike and I took his jet to Palm Beach, Florida, where we headed to an oceanside resort called Mar-a-Lago (for a brief time known, of course, as the Winter White House). The views were great and you could see a ton of water in most directions, but the resort itself looked a little run-down, and nicer from a distance.

It was a doubles tournament, and I was paired with the one and only Drew Gitlin, a former tennis pro. You've never heard of Drew Gitlin? You're in good company. Drew is a nice guy who once made it to a few pro doubles finals, but he really had no titles to his name. His ranking peaked at #58 in 1983, or sixteen years prior. Yet he was still young—about forty—and he was hungry.

"Hey," Drew said to me, "I'd really like to win this thing. Can you play?"

"Yeah, I'm a pretty decent player," I said. "But if you really want to win this thing, you should let me play in the ad court, because I'm left-handed."

For context, this was a bold request to make of a professional tennis player. Typically, the ad court is where the strongest player plays. Gitlin had every right to reject the idea.

"Sure," he said. "Happily."

The night before the start of play, at a glitzy dinner by the ocean, Trump and Milken hosted a Calcutta, which is basically an auction where anyone—tennis players, guests, CEOs, future presidents—could "purchase" a team, essentially placing a bet on that team to win the event. The proceeds of the Calcutta raised money for prostate cancer research. If you bought a team and your team won, you'd win a share of the proceeds.

Big money went to the big names. Just like at an auction, an emcee introduced each tennis legend with a dramatic flourish, listing all of their titles and records. "The former #1 women's player in the world, and the winner of three Grand Slams . . . Traaacy Austin!"

Someone bid $5,000, the minimum price, for Tracy's team.

"$10,000!"

"$15,000!"

"$20,000!"

The bids kept coming. Up and up and up, and the winning bid went for around $85,000.

Then came more Grand Slam winners, more former #1s in the world, more $50,000 bids.

The emcee, at last, came to our team. He looked carefully at his notes.

Drew and I made eye contact. This could get embarrassing.

"Drew Gitlin," the MC began, "who was voted, ah, 'Best Body on the Male Tour' by the women's tour.'"

Drew just laughed. Apparently he had a good body.

And everyone else remained silent. Dead silence. Not a single bid. Not the minimum $5,000, and I'm not sure that anyone was willing to bid $500 or even $5.

More silence.

"I'll buy our team," I said. "$5,000."

In the morning we won our first match. Our unconventional strategy—with me on the ad side, taking advantage of my lefty forehand—gave us an edge. Then we won our second match.

Thanks to a couple of lucky bounces that went our way, we won our third match, advanced to the quarterfinals, and faced a team anchored by Tracy Austin, the former #1 women's tennis player in the world . . . who partnered with Larry Tisch, then in his early eighties. Despite Austin's brilliance, Tisch was, well, in his eighties, and we took advantage of his limited mobility. We won easily.

Suddenly we found ourselves in the semifinals.

Waiting for us in the semis was Robert Seguso, the doubles specialist, who had won four Grand Slams and a litany of titles. He once beat Stefan Edberg to win a doubles' championship. Seguso was in top shape, still in his midthirties.

Seguso's partner?

Donald J. Trump.

Trump walked onto the red clay courts. This was a considerably fitter version of Donald than we're used to seeing today. He was dressed in tennis whites—white shorts, white polo shirt, white ball cap, and long white socks that almost reached his knees.

I shook hands with Trump before the match—there was no "death grip," at least not back then—and we began to warm up with a few easy ground strokes. From across the court, I could hear Seguso and Trump talking strategy.

"Hey," Seguso said to Trump, "you don't get here without being pretty good."

Trump nodded.

"So let's assume that we're tied up, at 4–all. We can't lose."

Seguso was referring to the fact that this was a handicapped tournament, and that each team had a certain number of "bisques," or free points. Team Trump had five bisques. We had two, so there was a net differential of three points. This meant that Team Trump could take three free points at any time during the match. The format was an eight-game pro set. If it went to 4–all there would be a tiebreaker, so it was essentially the first to five. Seguso's logic? If it got to 4–all, because of their three bisques, they had it in the bag.

The match began. Trump, or at least the 1999 version of Trump, was a respectable amateur tennis player. He was in decent shape. He knew strategy and he could hit the ball with pace and accuracy. At six foot one and maybe 190, 200 pounds, he had a solid presence at the net.

I forget what happened in the first few games—and for some reason ESPN didn't broadcast the match, so I can't watch a replay—but I know that it was a close set, and we pulled ahead 4 games to 3.

Team Trump's serve.

They had no margin for error. If we took this game, we won the match.

Deuce. Seguso's serve. He served to my partner, who smacked an outright winner in return.

Ad-out: advantage us.

This was now match point. And they still had a bisque. This should *clearly* have been a time to take a bisque. You literally can't imagine a more critical point.

Trump looked at Seguso. They made eye contact. *Bisque?*

Seguso held up his hand to say, *It's okay, I've got this.* They didn't take the bisque.

My turn to return the serve. Since the guy was blasting ninety-plus-mile-per-hour serves, I could either 1) wait to see which direction he served it, which would probably take too long and I'd get aced; or 2) guess. If I guessed right, I had a chance; if I guessed wrong, it would look pretty silly. I quickly strategized with Drew, "If I were him, I'd serve to my backhand."

"Absolutely. Just guess."

Seguso hit a clean, gorgeous, 100 mile-per-hour serve. No time to react. No time to make a decision. Yet I had guessed right, and the serve came straight to my backhand. We were on a clay court so it was a forgiving bounce. I hit one of the best two-handed backhands I'd ever hit in my life.

The ball rocketed over the net, waist-high . . . and shot straight toward Donald Trump's belt buckle. It hit his racket and knocked the racket out of his hand.

Trump lost his balance and fell on the red-brown clay, dirtying his pristine tennis whites.

The shot was a winner. Game over. Match over.

The reaction? Given what I had heard of him at the time, and given what we now know about Donald Trump, you might expect a tirade of profanity or a demand of an instant replay challenge.

Instead he just hopped right up. "Great shot!" Trump said. "What a shot. Holy mackerel! Congratulations."

Trump jogged to the net and shook my hand. His partner was less gracious; Seguso just did a 180 and sulked off the court.

In the finals, we beat Mike Milken and John Lloyd, winning the Calcutta. Oh, and because I had bought our team, given nobody else was interested, we won $100,000, which we happily gave to the charity. Not bad for a former pro that no one had heard of, matched with a former CEO most people had never heard of.

CHAPTER 10

Pay It Forward

Small gestures can have outsized impacts. This is especially true when you're in a position of seniority or power. The organizational psychologist and best-selling author Adam Grant has a concept called "The Five-Minute Favor," which is essentially that a small gesture from you can go a long way for others. "Giving doesn't require becoming Mother Teresa or Mahatma Gandhi," Grant once explained. "We can all find ways of adding high value to others' lives at a low personal cost."

Years and even decades before Adam Grant coined the term, my father mastered the art of the Five-Minute Favor (The Frank Favor?). On a deeper level, my father lived his life according to the maxim that "to whom much is given, much is expected." He might not have used those exact words, but he lived it. He attributed so much success—in his career and his life—to that generous break he caught when applying to Princeton in the 1960s, and from that moment, he felt compelled to give back. He paid it forward in so many ways.

His greatest contributions came from his eager willingness to help someone out, no matter how big or small the request. A quick call from him could have an extraordinary impact on someone's career, and he understood that. The Frank Favor could and did make careers, change lives, and launch companies and blockbuster movies.

This chapter is a little short because my father was so modest, and he didn't particularly care for sharing stories of him helping others. In previous chapters, you've already read examples of how willing he was to help others—including the story in the introduction about how he made one phone call that allowed *The Hangover* to be filmed at Caesars Palace in Las Vegas. Here's one more story from him about sharing his wisdom, then more stories from me and other third parties about seeing his generosity in action.

60 Minutes Indemnification

JANE

A bit of irony: Even though my father served as CEO for multiple companies, he was something of a cynic about corporations. This is partly because he uncovered fraud in not one but two occasions (TelePrompTer and Topper Toys). So here's a story where he was able to use his hard-won (if cynical) corporate wisdom to help out a friend, without expecting anything in return.

FRANK

In the early 1980s, we were living in Riverdale (a neighborhood in the Bronx, New York), and our neighbors would summer in Maine every year and rent out their homes. One of our neighbors had rented their home to George Crile.

George was a producer at *60 Minutes* of some note and tenure (and later the writer of *Charlie Wilson's War*), and had been the producer of a documentary on William Westmoreland and the Vietnam War titled *The Uncounted Enemy: A Vietnam Deception*. It contended some statistics had been manipulated to put the war and the US defense forces in a better light than the real numbers might have otherwise shown.

Westmoreland decided to sue CBS. He named the head of *60 Minutes*, the head correspondent (Mike Wallace), and George Crile as defendants, among others. I followed the trial because George was a friend.

One day George had a summer cocktail party for his colleagues at CBS, and some of their neighbors in Riverdale. I asked George how he felt the trial was going, because it seemed—just by reading the press—that the Westmoreland argument was beginning to gain some strength and that CBS was increasingly on the defensive.

George said no, he thought it was going fine.

"Are you represented by CBS, or do you have your own counsel?" I asked him.

George said that the CBS counsel was representing all parties, including himself.

I said, "You know, George, I'm a cynic about corporations in general. When they find themselves in a position where they may be in jeopardy of losing, or have damages found against them, they would be willing to compromise. That's generally by blaming the low person on the totem pole . . . which seems to be you." I had learned this myself, many years ago, when the firm tried to blame me for the irregularities at Topper Toys, as I was then the junior guy on the totem pole.

He shook his head. "No, no, no, this is a long-standing team here at CBS, and I don't think that's going to be an issue."

George went back to the party. Two hours later he wandered up to me looking somewhat perturbed, and said, "Look, I can't get out of my head what we were talking about. And I'm not sure what to do."

I said, "Well, my outside lawyer is Arthur Liman, who's at Paul Weiss. I could ask him if he'd be prepared to talk about whether you needed your own personal counsel or not."

He thought about it. He came back again and said, "If you'd make that call, I would really appreciate it. I would just like some cold comfort."

So I called Arthur and he said, "Sure, have him give me a buzz."

George eventually called Arthur and explained to him what was transpiring, and what his situation was vis-a-vis the other CBS defendants in the trial. I don't know exactly what Arthur told him, but he said, in effect, "Let me speak to the CBS general counsel."

To this day, I'm not entirely sure precisely what was said in their conversation, but the net effect was that George came out with, essentially, an indemnification from CBS: They wouldn't try to point fingers at him, or lay whatever blame there was to lay on the junior guy on the totem pole. The trial then went on with its own natural course and was settled a few years later.[11]

Philanthropy with a Capital P

Dad was fiercely committed to philanthropy, supporting worthy causes, and using his money and his network to help those less fortunate, particularly children. This spanned years. Over many decades, he and my mother raised and donated funds for a wide range of organizations, and in particular a social services agency in New York City, Rising Ground (previously known as Leake & Watts). Rising Ground named a school after my parents, The Carol and Frank Biondi Education Center, or, as it's now known: The Biondi School. When my husband and I visited the campus a few years ago, it was an inspiration to see the students that never met him—never knew *of* him—be so directly impacted by his generous spirit.

Less directly, but just as impactful, he gave to his alma maters to help those who came after him, including Harvard and Princeton. At Princeton, he was elected to serve as an alumni trustee. He served on the board (he was always serving on boards) when the board made the decision to eliminate loans from student financial aid packages, turning them into grants that would never need to be repaid. "The board's goal," he would tell me, "is to make it less expensive for a

---

11 *Westmoreland v. CBS*, Wikipedia, accessed April 19, 2022, https://en.wikipedia.org/wiki/
Westmoreland_v._CBS.

student from Iowa with modest means to attend Princeton than the University of Iowa." And he helped make that happen.

That legacy lives on to this day. In the January 2021 edition of the *Princeton Alumni Weekly*, the current president of the university, Christopher Ludwig Eisgruber, spelled out the impact of this change, how moving toward grants instead of loans allowed graduates not to be encumbered by debt, "opening [Princeton's] gates to talented young people who would previously have found the University unaffordable."

This move at Princeton had a ripple effect across higher education. As Eisgruber noted in the *Alumni Weekly*, twenty years ago, the president of Columbia Teachers College said in *The New York Times*, "Every Ivy League University is going to have to try to match this if they want to compete for the best of the middle-class students." That's exactly what happened. That was part of Princeton's (and the Trustees) plan. Eisgruber credited Princeton's "no loan" approach as being a "defining benchmark for financial aid programs," noting that over twenty institutions of higher learning provided grants that met the full need of all of their students, and that a much larger number of colleges and universities provided full funding to students facing financial hardship. Then he specifically cites the role of those who made it possible. "I am profoundly conscious that Princeton's alumni and friends were the driving force behind the 2001 decision to go 'no loan' and the tremendous good that has followed from that change," wrote Eisgruber. "By paying it forward to new generations of students, you have improved their lives, enhanced our University, and raised the aspirations of institutions throughout our country."[12]

My father was proud of the university's bold leadership. He felt privileged to have had a small hand in making it happen. He understood that talent was distributed equally across the country (and the

---

12 Christopher L. Eisgruber, "Twenty Years Later: Princeton's Visionary Financial Aid Program," *Princeton Alumni Weekly*, January 2021.

world), but opportunity was not. So he did what he could to give others the same opportunity he was given.

I won't list them all, but there are so many examples of his philanthropic leadership and generosity. He chaired the capital campaign to raise money for a new hospital, endowed a scholarship fund at the school where my sister and I both attended, and supported too many charities to count.

Giving Started at Home

While these grand gestures are what often gets noticed by the outside world, Dad's generosity played out in many smaller ways, starting at home. He did so much for us—for my sister, for me, for his grandchildren. I have a vivid memory of my college application process. This was the mid-'90s, when applications needed to be completed on specific forms by hand or on typewriters. But since we used computers for all of our school work, I wanted to use a computer to complete my applications: an early Mac laptop, the kind that looked a bit like a futuristic waffle iron and weighed just as much.

We were still a long way away from a digital common application for colleges, but thankfully, some enterprising software companies digitized universities' college applications, so applicants could complete them on a computer. I bought that software for my Mac. So far so good . . . until it came time to submit them. The internet was still in its dial-up stone age, so the only way to file the applications was to print them out.

Just one problem: I was nowhere near a Mac printer. They were much harder to find than printers for PCs. We were on Christmas vacation, and Dad had just been released from a few (scary) days in the hospital with a bout of pneumonia. Despite his own fragile, recovering health, he drove me to multiple Kinko's locations in a frantic hunt for a Mac with a printer. We just barely managed to find one, print out the remaining applications, and race to the post office with a few hours to spare. Even when coughing and weak, he did whatever it took to help his family.

Opening the Door

JANE

I have many stories how my father used his position to help other people. As in other things, he downplayed the role, but the impact on the lives of those involved was tremendous.

One of my favorite stories in this category starts with the Mets. I was a big-time Mets fan growing up. I can still clearly remember the 1986 World Series, which cemented my fandom. That team's first-base coach was named Bill Robinson.

My father was introduced to Bill shortly after that World Series. They became friendly, and I had the chance to meet him as well. A few years later, Bill was kind enough to give me former MLB All-Star Lenny Dykstra's last bat as a New York Met, before Dykstra was traded to the Phillies. (I still own that bat.) And around the same time, Bill's eldest son, Bill Jr., was graduating from college and looking for a job.

So my dad did what he often did—he gave someone a chance. He arranged for Bill Robinson Jr. to meet with Tom Freston (then the head of MTV), which led to a job in ad sales at MTV. Bill Jr. made the most of the opportunity, he impressed the execs at MTV, and he went on to have a successful career in ad sales at NBC and Fox Sports. After my father passed away, Bill Jr. wrote me the nicest note, saying what an important person my father was in his life.

This note has some surprising symmetry. When I graduated from business school, I interned with the New York Mets. Finally I was earning the big bucks: they paid me minimum wage, $5.15 per hour, which meant that every day I debated whether I wanted to splurge to pay the toll and drive through the midtown tunnel, or spend the extra time driving over the Queensborough bridge, because it was free. (I usually went with the bridge.)

Because they shared the same division, the Mets played the Marlins often, and during their first series that season I was delighted to see the Marlins' hitting coach: Bill Robinson Sr. It turns out that Bill Sr. won two World Series rings as a hitting coach—one in '86 with the Mets, and one in '03 with the Marlins. We laughed and caught up, and he knew I was determined to work in baseball full time, so he offered to share my resume with the Marlins and put in a good word.

A few months passed. I never did end up interviewing with the Marlins, but I did land a full-time marketing job with the Dodgers. And then one day Bill Robinson Sr. called my desk and said, "Surprise! One of our coworkers told me you worked here!" It turns out he was now a coach in the Dodgers' minor league system. We laughed and again caught up; by this time I had known him for nearly twenty years.

Later that season, while on a road trip for the Dodgers, Bill Robinson Sr. died in his sleep. I wrote his wife Mary a sympathy note, and she wrote me back the most thoughtful and inspiring letter. I still have the letter, and it brought me comfort to re-read when my own father passed. "I must agree with you, I can't imagine Bill not being here," Mary wrote. "I'm not without hope, I know I will see him again in heaven."

And Dad never made a fuss about how he helped others. "Your father told me that he only 'opened' the door and the rest would be up to me—downplaying the influence the chair and CEO of Viacom would have in the internal decision-making process," Bill told me recently. "Typical Frank Biondi."

Knowledge Given Freely

JANE

Dad didn't just open doors for deserving people. He often freely shared his hard-won knowledge with others. Including with Dr. Phil in the early days of his now decades-long successful daytime talk show.

Dr. Phil moved to LA in the early 2000s, and this is when he met my father on the tennis court. Normally, as Dr. Phil describes it, after a typical Sunday tennis match, people chat for a few minutes and then they get in their cars and drive home. Not Dr. Phil and my father. After matches they would speak for hours. Sometimes about their families, sometimes on deeper values and philosophy (more on that later), and sometimes about Dr. Phil's budding TV aspirations. This was before Dr. Phil was a household name. At the time, he didn't know the ins and outs of the TV industry.

Guess who taught him? "He was incredibly helpful to me," says Dr. Phil, as my father gave him a master class on how to understand "the players on the chessboard." Dad took all of that accumulated wisdom from decades in the television industry—from TelePrompTer to HBO to MTV—and unleashed it as free advice. My father broke down the tricky relationships between networks, studios, affiliates, and the "O&Os" (owned-and-operated stations). He demystified the bottom line, explaining who had leverage. "He gave me a tremendous amount of insight about the business," says Dr. Phil. "The only thing he wanted was for me to understand how it worked. He didn't ask for anything in return. He would just talk for hours about these insights. Who does that?"

These small gestures would often lead to friendships that lasted years and decades, and sometimes spanned generations. My mom used to joke that Dad should have kept track of every time he fulfilled a request or favor, because he could have cashed in on them countless times, but he almost never did. And now, decades later, Bill Jr.'s wife and I are colleagues by sheer coincidence; one of those coincidences that makes you believe that you must be in the right place, that the universe or whatever higher power you believe in is conspiring in your favor. And now that Dad is no longer with us, moments like that give me special comfort.

He gave to others because it was the right thing to do, because others gave to him, and because it gave him great satisfaction to make a difference in other people's lives. It led others, including me, to follow his example—to be like Frank—and this is a noble and lasting legacy that he left behind.

CHAPTER 11

Define What Success Means to You

For most of my life, I heard many of my father's stories and I could point to the highlights of his career, but at the same time, I always wanted to know and understand him as a person, beyond just what he did at work. Despite all his public successes and triumphs, at home he was shy and reserved.

I remember one attempt to get to know him better. One Christmas after I graduated from college, I bought two copies of a book, *All About Me: The Story of Your Life: Guided Journal*, and it's packed with questions and prompts for jotting down personal details about yourself, ranging from the easy stuff (your favorite color, favorite sport) to the more philosophical (your fears, your emotions, your toughest choices).

I thought we could each fill out our own copy with our answers, swap books, and then we'd learn more about each other in a way that he might feel more comfortable sharing.

A week went by, then two, then three. It soon became clear that Dad had no intention of filling out the book, or even telling me that he wouldn't. He never brought it up. Sometime later, we had a disagreement or difficult conversation, I don't remember what it was about, but I brought up the book and his reluctance to communicate.

"Why are you so reluctant to open up?" I asked him. "Why don't you ever want to talk about these things?"

"I'm reluctant to share my opinion," he said, "because I don't want to sway your decisions." He said he wanted me to make my own choices, to learn on my own.

But I pushed back. "Dad, it would be really nice to know how you feel about these things." Disappointed, I told him that I had made an effort to try to connect, and he had essentially ignored the gesture. I thought that was the end of the conversation. I dropped it.

Two years later I went to Sydney, Australia, to study abroad during business school, and I received an email from my dad. The email contained a few of the book's questions, along with some thoughtful answers. A week later I received another email—more questions, more answers. Nearly every week while I was away, he sent me questions and answers from *All About Me*. It was easier for him to share these things with me in writing, while I was halfway around the world, than it was to do in person. When he was pushed to realize this exchange was important to me, he found the strength to work through his own discomfort, and he did it, in a way that he felt comfortable.

That last concept is something I think about often. Succeeding in life is often about getting comfortable with discomfort. We're not trained for that. Fundamentally, and especially as Americans, we mostly believe that life should be happy-go-lucky and easy. But often it's not. Sometimes we need to find the joy amid the muck or break out of our comfort zone to persevere and help others . . . and that's what Dad did for me. Yet even after those lovely exchanges of emails, I always knew there was more to know and understand about my father.

Then everything changed when he became ill. In 2018, my father was diagnosed with stage-four advanced urothelial cancer—life-threatening bladder cancer. He fought it with dignity and determination. As with everything he did, he impressed all the doctors and nurses as he withstood chemotherapy, immunotherapy, and a new experimental treatment. I never heard him complain until the end of his life.

I suppose that no one truly prepares for their parents' mortality, but with Dad it was especially jarring. He'd always been so vigorous. As recently as in 2016, my daughter and I joined him at his fiftieth college reunion at Princeton. Many of his classmates—in their early seventies—were driven around in golf carts. And he walked around fit as a fiddle. At the time I told him, "Dad, I promise, when we're at your seventy-fifth reunion, I'll drive your golf cart." That would be when he was ninety-six, and I meant it.

"No way," he said. "I'll be walking."

In his mind he would still be a spry ninety-six-year-old, perhaps ready for a doubles tennis match, and I let his mindset anchor my own. Why wouldn't he be a healthy ninety-something?

Then, reality.

For so many years in his career, he accomplished much by his own hard work, clear-eyed analysis, and sound judgment. Then the cancer arrived. Soon he could no longer ignore it, and he couldn't try to do it all on his own.

His initial treatment cycles lasted three weeks. Each three-week period included two hours-long infusions of all his medications, with roughly a week at the end to recover before the next one began. It went like this from late summer through Christmas. When I was in Los Angeles, I was able to take him to one of those treatments in the fall, giving my mom a break and spending the day with him. He refused to get a chemo port (which makes it easier for them to inject the medicine), so they would have to poke him a few times to get a vein. Apparently he was a tough stick.

The chemotherapy helped him. The cancer appeared to retreat, and he was even feeling strong enough to play the occasional round of golf in the winter and spring. His chemo ended and he continued with the immunotherapy treatment. His spirits remained high. "I had a relatively good experience with chemo," he said at one point. "I didn't have nausea. I didn't lose my hair, even though they said I'd lose my hair." He acknowledged his energy was lower, but said, "Other than that, it's like, you know, set 'em up, knock 'em down, set 'em up, knock 'em down." Or in other words, even now, even in his final chapter: Do the work.

The Lesson I Wish I Could Have Taught Him

JANE

While of course I admire and deeply respect my father's fighting spirit, I also, at times, wonder if he could have been a better advocate for himself. He was always so giving, so unwilling to make a fuss, and so content to have that "inner sense of accomplishment" (as Alan Schwartz once put it), that he rarely spoke up for himself. He rarely acknowledged pain. This was even true in his career, when he refused to hold grudges after being fired, whether at HBO or Viacom or Universal; he just dusted himself off, shrugged, and moved on to the next adventure. That worked for him.

But while I've spent a lifetime of appreciating and accepting my father's advice, there is the one bit of counsel I wish I could have given to him, or that he would have been willing to hear: **It's okay to be your own advocate**. Ninety-nine percent of the stories in Dad's amazing life give the reader something to emulate, but this is one where, I hope, you can see some merit in a path he didn't take, especially when it comes to facing your own mortality. It's also the piece of advice I give to those I know that are fighting cancer or any other major medical obstacle.

By late spring of 2019, Dad's scans showed that the cancer was growing again. They would need to try something new. The doctors said he was a candidate for a brand new drug for his exact condition, just approved by the FDA a month before. We were all hopeful.

But there was no miracle cure.

A Lasting Legacy

JANE

If there was a silver lining to his battle with cancer, it was that it allowed us to grieve and prepare for his loss—as much as one can prepare for such a thing. We talked about his expectations, I asked uncomfortable questions, and he gave thoughts on how to help my mom when he was gone.

And we also discussed a book. This book. After years of nudging him to write a book about his career, when he got sick, I chose to force the issue. When his diagnosis proved to be the worst-case scenario, we all cried. We talked about how he would battle the disease. And then I said, "Now you have to write this book."

"I had the same thought," Dad said.

So we spent the next year recording his stories and reflections, exploring the arc of his extraordinary career, and thinking more about the lessons and values he wanted to share.

He was never able to finish that book. My father passed away on Monday, November 25, 2019.

A few weeks before he died, I was with him in his hospital room. I started tearing up and my voice started to crack. He told me to stop crying, and I told him that it made me sad to see him suffer. He said matter-of-factly, as he always did, "Nothing lasts forever." Which only made me want to cry more. He was right that time is precious, and it's promised to no one. It gives me comfort to think that if he had been offered a trade—the incredible life he led, but it would have to end too soon, when it did . . . he might have taken that deal.

At the funeral, when I delivered Dad's eulogy, I made a promise to the hundreds of his friends and family members and beloved colleagues who came to celebrate his life: I would help him complete his final project. Finishing his book felt like the best way to honor his legacy, and the right way to spread his values and principles beyond the upper echelons of the media business—and to all of the entrepreneurs, executives (current and future), and professionals who could benefit from his wisdom.

For months I sat with my father's stories. I studied them, I heard his calming voice in my head, and I tried to snap all the pieces of the puzzle together. I did this during the depths of COVID-19 quarantine, while also working at my day job, grieving along with my mom and sister, and also raising my own daughter—the youngest of my father's six grandchildren.

Finishing the book helped me grieve. It helped me understand *him* better. And it helped me understand *me* better. Exploring these key moments of his life—and examining the way he made decisions— gave me a better perspective on my own journey. When I finished, I realized that his stories offer all of us some principles for how to be a better leader, a better partner, a better person.

His lessons are simple but powerful. He took both HBO and Viacom to new heights with a formula that focused on empowering others, partnering for the long term (and giving both sides some wins in negotiations), doing the work, and living with integrity.

One Last Lesson

Over a year after he passed, in a surprising twist, I gleaned one final insight about his values and sense of purpose. I learned this through one of my father's closest friends in the last two decades of his life, Dr. Phil. The two had grown close, spending hour after hour on the tennis courts, and then countless hours in deep conversation.

After Dad learned that the cancer diagnosis could be terminal, he opened up even further to Dr. Phil. "We had conversations that I don't think he had with anybody else in his life," Dr. Phil said recently. "He was very philosophical." I learned that Dad spoke to Dr. Phil about his values, his family, his sense of purpose, his legacy—essentially, the guts of this very book. And I was moved to learn what he had said.

"The job of the parent is to prepare your children for their next level of life," my father told Dr. Phil toward the end. Dad continued:

"When you've done that, when you feel like your kids and your family have become self-sufficient, you've done your job." There it is, that unbroken theme of Dad's: doing your job. My father was at peace with what, in his mind, was life's most important job.

As Dr. Phil relayed, my father then elaborated: "I feel like if I'm going to exit this world, I really do feel like I've done my job. I will pass the world with peace in my heart, because I've done my job and everyone's in a good place." He then said something that channels the spirit of this book we wrote together: "You pass along the things you value, and leave behind the things you don't, and I think we have a good generational legacy."

He then went one step further. "What a gift they [my family] have given me. By being who they were," my father said to Dr. Phil, who then wanted to underscore this point, repeating it several times.

"He didn't just say, 'I've done my job,'" Dr. Phil said. "He said, 'What a gift they've given me, by being who they are.' It wasn't about him, it was about them. What greater gift can you get than seeing your children flourish? So he could be at peace."

And what a gift my father gave me with that sentiment, in some ways spoken from beyond the grave. Talk about finding value.

My father's sense of this ultimate purpose—living life on his terms, and passing along his values—reminds me of the advice he shared with me, long ago, on how to frame and define success. "There are many ways to define achievement," he would tell me, cautioning that too often we let others, or society, do the defining. He would remind me that I need to have my own sense of purpose, "otherwise you'll always be chasing someone else's rainbow."

My father lived a rich life full of purpose, and this earned him the highest levels of success. But success needn't look like running HBO, or investing in Castle Rock, or sitting on the board of directors.

Although I work in a different industry in a smaller and less visible job, it wasn't until I experienced corporate America for myself that I came to appreciate the scale, scope, and impact of his accomplishments. His sickness and untimely death has focused my attention (perhaps morbidly) on what I most want to be known for.

I want to be valued as a team player, a voice of reason, a truth-teller, and the person others want to work and be with. And I've learned from my father's management style. I pride myself on being a "human first" manager. I want for my employees what they want for themselves. In other words, I strive to position their work so that, yes, we accomplish the goal, but also so that each team member can learn, grow, develop the skills they care about, and make progress on their own career's journey.

In his final gift, my father gave me this last lesson: Through this very book, he has reminded me of my own sense of purpose. In something of a paradox, understanding his story has given me new perspective on my own story, my own values, my own goals in both career and life. I don't need to emulate his journey. I just need to make the best of mine. I can follow his wisdom, incorporate his guidance, and use it to find my own rainbow.

I hope he's inspired you to do the same.

The Math of Discount Rates

Given my father's background as an investment banker, it should come as no surprise that many of the stories in the book relate to evaluating whether an investment that a company is considering is worth it. Case in point: Should Coca-Cola buy Embassy pictures at a price tag of $500 million? (See chapter 3 for the full story.)

The math comes down to this: you estimate a company's profits and losses **in the future,** then use a **discount rate** (the reverse of a "rate of return") to tell you what that future value is worth today ("present value"). That discount rate is critical in determining whether you should spend money today in anticipation of future return.

The formula for doing the calculation to determine the present value is shown here.

$$PV = FV / (1 + r)^n$$

PV = present value

FV = future value

r = rate of return (aka discount rate)

n = number of periods of time

$(1+r)^n$ means you multiply (1 + discount rate) by itself n number of times. For example, if $(1+r)$ = 1.03 and n = 5, then that part of the equation would mean (1.03 x 1.03 x 1.03 x 1.03 x 1.03) = 1.159.

Using a simplified example, let's suppose you expect an investment to be worth $100 five years from now. That is, FV= $100 and n = 5. The formula looks like this:

$$PV = 100 \, / \, (1 + r)^5$$

The question, then, is what r or discount rate you want to use. The lower the rate, the lower the fraction's denominator, and the less the value is "discounted."

For the sake of illustration, let's say an investment is relatively safe and we'll give it a lower r value of 3 percent. To estimate the value today of something that is worth $100 five years into the future, the calculation looks like this:

$$\$100 \, / \, (1 + .03)^5 = \$100 \, / \, 1.159 = \$86$$

If the investment is considered risky, the r value can get quite high because of the uncertainty. So for comparison, let's use an r value of 20 percent:

$$\$100 \, / \, (1 + .20)^5 = \$100 \, / \, 2.488 = \$40$$

For a relatively safe investment that only has to return 3 percent a year, you're OK putting in $86 with an expected value of it being worth $100 in five years. If the investment is riskier, the expected rate of return has to be higher in order for you to be confident in the investment. And in this case, that would mean not spending more than $40 for that expected value of $100 in the future.

In short, how much you should invest today varies a lot by how safe you think that investment is and what you expect it will be worth in the future. Just as slight changes in interest rates to your credit card loan or your mortgage can make a massive impact to what you owe, this is also the case with billion-dollar transactions.

In the example given in chapter 3, the question on the table was whether Coca-Cola should invest $500 million to buy Embassy pictures. By delving into Embassy's cash flow, my father came up with an estimate of the company's Future Value (FV) five years out ($n = 5$).

Initially, the CFO of Coke told Dad to use a discount rate (r) of 16 percent. Plugging the values into the question, Dad estimated the present value (PV) of Embassy to be only $355 million at that discount rate—well below the $500 million asking price—with that discount rate of 16 percent.

When Dad made the argument that the TV revenues were far less risky than the movie revenues—and therefore deserved a lower discount rate—he was allowed to adjust the discount rate down for a portion of the cash flow . . . and ended up with a present value of about $500 million for Embassy, and Coke's purchase of Embassy went through. As discussed in chapter 3, Dad's approach proved to be sound, and Coke securitized those same licensing fees at a favorable rate shortly thereafter, netting the company hundreds of millions of dollars.

Acknowledgments

In addition to those who shared firsthand stories and experiences, there are others who made valuable contributions to complete this project.

Thanks to my cousin William for his inspiration for the title. *Let Me Be Frank* would have been the title had Dad lived long enough to publish it himself, so we pivoted to the similar *Let's Be Frank* instead. Thanks, William. I'll never forget the family dinner when your brilliant idea captured Dad's attention, brought a smile to his face, and improved the title instantly.

Thank you to John Schmidt, Tony Schwartz, Skip Stein, Blair Westlake, William Cohan, and Randy Strickley for reading early drafts and giving me feedback on the book and helpful advice and direction on ways to move the project forward. Thanks to Eric Rayman for his guidance and input. Thanks to Rob Weisbach and Scott Miller for their help early on.

Thanks to Alex Berliner for his permission to use his wonderful photograph. Thanks to Annie Leibovitz / Trunk collective and the Associated Press for licensing their images, and to John Plunkett for his *Wired* cover artwork.

I'd like to express my gratitude to the team at River Grove books for their time and expertise finishing the project and publishing it.

Thanks in particular to: Lee Reed Zarnikau, Sue Reynard, and Pam Nordberg for their input, hard work, and dedication; Brian Phillips for the design; Jen Glynn for keeping us on track.

Thanks to Dad's many doctors for helping him fight long enough to capture what he intended to share in this book. A final acknowledgment to my dad for pushing past his initial hesitance to pursue this. Sharing his perspective and experiences was the ultimate gift he could give us at the end of his life. Thanks, Dad. We miss you so much.

About the Authors

Frank Biondi (1945–2019)

Name a company in the entertainment business and there's a good chance Frank Biondi ran it: HBO. Viacom. Universal. The full list goes on for a while, and it includes overseeing channels and assets that are household names like MTV, Nickelodeon, Showtime, *Wheel of Fortune*, and *Jeopardy!*

AP Photo / Beth A. Keiser

Over a remarkable forty-year career spanning from the late 1960s into the 2000s, Biondi served—quietly, and rarely in the spotlight—as one of the most prolific CEOs in all of media. As the head of HBO, Biondi doubled the company's subscribers from eight million to sixteen million. When he arrived, it was losing money; when he left, it made an annual $180 million.

He led Viacom and MTV through their '90s glory years. A glowing, thirteen-thousand-word *New Yorker* profile described Biondi as "Sumner Redstone's secret weapon," concluding that "Redstone bought Viacom, but Biondi is the one who has built it." Under Biondi's watch,

Viacom's profits surged from $300 million to $2 billion, and *Fortune* named it the second-most-admired media company in the United States.

As the CEO of Universal, Biondi ran a movie business, a theme park, and a TV studio that grew *Law & Order* into a juggernaut.

He served on over twenty corporate boards, including Amgen, Hasbro, Madison Square Garden, Maybelline, StubHub, Vail Resorts, Viacom, Yahoo!, and the Bank of New York Mellon. He also served on the board of trustees of Princeton University, from which he graduated in 1966. In addition, he earned an MBA from Harvard Business School.

Jane Biondi Munna

Courtesy Alex J. Bertiner / ABImages

Jane Biondi Munna is an executive at one of the nation's largest financial institutions. She has served for over a decade in roles across marketing, finance, strategy, and communications, including as the executive communications partner to the co-president and COO of the firm.

Her career has spanned finance, media, and sports. Jane can talk corporate "inside baseball," and she can also talk "baseball baseball." Her twenty years of experience—which, like her father, also began with investment banking—included a few years in marketing and special events for the Los Angeles Dodgers where she booked celebrities to throw out the ceremonial first pitch or sing the national anthem and coordinated pregame and in-game entertainment for corporate sponsorship partners. On Opening Day in 2007, Jane and her team delighted Dodgers fans with a surprise appearance by a young (and, at the time up-and-coming) talent named Taylor Swift. Jane is a behind-the-scenes doer and connector of people and ideas. In other words . . . her father's daughter.

She earned an MBA from the UCLA Anderson School of Management and a BA from Princeton.

CPSIA information can be obtained
at www.ICGtesting.com
Printed in the USA
LVHW100633010323
740518LV00003B/69